Talking is for All

A Lucky Duck Book

I dedicate this book to my family, with love.

Talking is for All

How Children and Teenagers Develop Emotional Literacy

Betty Rudd

Los Angeles • London • New Delhi • Singapore

First published 2008

Apart from any fair dealing for the purposes of research or private study, or criticism or review, as permitted under the Copyright, Designs and Patents Act, 1988, this publication may be reproduced, stored or transmitted in any form, or by any means, only with the prior permission in writing of the publishers, or in the case of reprographic reproduction, in accordance with the terms of licences issued by the Copyright Licensing Agency. Enquiries concerning reproduction outside those terms should be sent to the publishers.

All material on the accompanying CD Rom can be printed off and photocopied by the purchaser/user of the book. The CD Rom itself may not be reproduced in its entirety for use by others without prior written permission from SAGE. The CD Rom may not be distributed or sold separately from the book without the prior written permission of SAGE. Should anyone wish to use the materials from the CD Rom for conference purposes, they would require separate permission from us. All material is © 2008

SAGE Publications Ltd
1 Oliver's Yard
55 City Road
London EC1Y 1SP

SAGE Publications Inc.
2455 Teller Road
Thousand Oaks, California 91320

SAGE Publications India Pvt Ltd
B 1/I 1 Mohan Cooperative Industrial Area
Mathura Road, Post Bag 7
New Delhi 110 044

SAGE Publications Asia-Pacific Pte Ltd
33 Pekin Street #02-01
Far East Square
Singapore 048763

Library of Congress Control Number 2008929345

British Library Cataloguing in Publication data

A catalogue record for this book is available from the British Library

ISBN 978-1-4129-3534-0 (pbk)

Illustrators: Dee Mills, Elizabeth A. Rennison, Ursula Graham-White

Typeset by C&M Digitals (P) Ltd., Chennai, India
Printed in India at Replika Pvt. Ltd
Printed on paper from sustainable resources

Contents

CD Contents vi
Acknowledgement ix
Preface x
About the author xii

Introduction and structural overview 1
Emotional literacy overview 3
How to use the resources 17

Part One   Talking is for Kids: Emotional literacy for 19
4–7 year olds
Introduction 20
Record keeping and assessment 21
Stories and activities 24
Plans for using the worksheets 30
Worksheets 38

Part Two   Talking is for Us: Emotional literacy for 63
8–12 year olds
Introduction 64
Record keeping and assessment 65
Stories and activities 68
Plans for using the worksheets 78
Worksheets 84

Part Three   Talking is for Teens: Emotional literacy for 111
13–19 year olds
Introduction 112
Record keeping and assessment 114
Stories and activities 116
Plans for using the worksheets 138
Worksheets 139

References 179
List of useful resources 183
Subject index 184
Resources index 186

CD Contents

Part One   Talking is for Kids (4–7 year olds)
Introduction
Assessment form
My record

Stories
Story 1   Jerry goes shopping
Story 2   Monique and her kitten
Story 3   Clever Thomas
Story 4   Peter in the playground
Story 5   Isabella had a friend

Plans for worksheets
Plans for using worksheets 1 to 18
Plan for using worksheet 4   Talking isn't medicine
Plan for using worksheet 6   You can feel bad if …
Plan for using worksheet 8   You can feel bad because …
Plan for using worksheet 9   You feeling good
Plan for using worksheet 10   Five ways to feel good
Plan for using worksheet 11   Healthy mind and body
Plan for using worksheet 12   Grow strong and healthy
Plan for using worksheet 13   Play with friends
Plan for using worksheet 14   Grow and heal
Plan for using worksheet 15   Be happy
Plan for using worksheet 16   Your feelings
Plan for using worksheet 17   Balance your life
Plan for using worksheet 18   Be kind to yourself
Plan for using worksheet 23   Feel secure in setting
Plan for using worksheet 24   Gain sense of self-worth

Part Two   Talking is for Us (8–12 year olds)
Introduction
Assessment form
My record

Stories
Story 1   Cecil and the little creature
Story 2   Yoko and the bully
Story 3   The twin
Story 4   Pollyanna's ninth birthday
Story 5   The school hamster

Plans for worksheets

Plan for using worksheet 3   Favourite pet
Plan for using worksheet 6   Let's talk
Plan for using worksheet 8   Recognise feelings
Plan for using worksheet 9   The present
Plan for using worksheet 10   Liking and smiling
Plans for using worksheets A to R   Belinda gets help
Plan for using worksheet S

Worksheets

Worksheet 1   Record of assessment
Worksheet 2   Achievement
Worksheet 3   Favourite pet
Worksheet 4   Let's talk
Worksheet 5   Recognise feelings
Worksheet 6   The present
Worksheet 7   Liking and smiling
Worksheets A-S

Part Three   Talking is for Teens (13–19 year olds)

Introduction
Assessment form

Stories

Story 1   Smoking
Story 2   Drug abuse
Story 3   Pregnancy
Story 4   Dropping out
Story 5   Violence
Story 6   Disease
Story 7   Impulse control
Story 8   Managing anger
Story 9   A solution to a predicament
Story 10   Sadness
Story 11   Jealousy
Story 12   Pride
Story 13   Guilt
Story 14   Anxiety
Story 15   Alcohol

Plans for using the worksheets

Worksheet 1   Creativity
Worksheet 2   Responsibility
Worksheet 3   Sad
Worksheet 4   Controlling yourself
Worksheet 5   Self-control
Worksheet 6   Problem solving
Worksheet 7   Teen + 10 years

Worksheet 8   Positive response to a negative comment
Worksheet 9   My contact
Worksheet 10   My life story
Worksheet 11   Impulse control
Worksheet 12   Managing anger
Worksheet 13   Choices
Worksheet 14   Positive
Worksheet 15   Lonely
Worksheet 16   Matching emotions
Worksheet 17   Self-booster
Worksheet 18   Affirmations
Worksheet 19   Self-concept
Worksheet 20   Understand and manage emotions
Worksheet 21   Communication
Worksheet 22   Compliments
Worksheet 23   Co-operation

Activities relating to Zak's story
Section 1–10 activities

Acknowledgements

I am grateful to my parents who taught me love and forgiveness.

My children, I thank you for being you, your forgiveness of my mistakes and for all you teach me, whether wittingly or unwittingly.

Thank you my sister Mary for your encouragement about my aspirations and for being there for me.

Special thanks go to the pupils and students of the schools and colleges in Sussex, and to my young clients, who were involved in the suggestions I thought of; irrespective of whether these are included or excluded within this publication.

Thank you Sage for wanting me to write this second edition of the *Talking is ...* series.

Particular thanks go to Barbara Maines and George Robinson who unfailingly supported me in conducting the whole 'Talking is ...' project; thank you so much for your feedback George, which as you will see, I have taken on board!

I also thank the artists who managed to flesh out my match-stick drawings, into the illustrations printed in *Talking is for All*.

Chartered Counselling Psychologist Joan Moore, thanks for your supervision for over the last decade, which continues.

Thank you Pro Vice Chancellor Professor Mary Watts, you enabled me to realise the value of focussing on and finishing one project at a time.

Heartfelt thanks to my husband Steve, without whom my life would not be so rich and enhanced in the love I nestle in which enables me to write.

Preface

This book is intended to make the learning and use of emotional literacy easy and enjoyable for children and teenagers. My main aims are to define emotional literacy and offer relevant hands-on activities that I have found and still find useful in my work with young individuals, while bearing in mind findings from relevant investigations. By developing youngsters' emotional literacy their emotional intelligence is raised, thus increasing their emotional quotient. The terms 'emotional literacy', 'emotional intelligence' and 'emotional quotient' (EQ), are not used interchangeably within this book, since they have different meanings. Emotional literacy refers to the amount a person has learnt regarding how she or he deals with her or his emotions. Emotional intelligence refers to the intelligent use of emotions, that is, emotional acumen. EQ refers to the amount of emotional intelligence within an individual.

Facilitating good mental health is very rewarding yet it can become an arduous task. It behoves each of us involved in supporting youngsters, to work out practices and principles enabling them to flourish in a healthier way. I hope that *Talking is for All* goes some way towards furthering that enabling process. It explains the reasons for aiding emotional literacy but does not solve every problem that a child or teenager faces. Rather, it provides guidelines to use as a yardstick for each young person, and a way of solving problems with regard to emotional literacy.

Although robust psychological health is linked to high emotional literacy, research is meagre on this point. Unfortunately, most of the research seems unsophisticated in its methods. However, an exemplary piece of good enough research was undertaken by Noeker and Petermann (1998). They investigated young people up to the age of 18 years. The outcome of this research showed that negative emotions were precipitating factors to ill physical health. 'The three emotions with the highest loadings were disappointment – loneliness – fear' (p.27). Indeed, they found that these three factors increased the likelihood of asthma; while strong support from father and mother was most relevant in a decreased likelihood of asthma. It is important to respond to findings such as these. *Talking is for All* is a response. However, more interventions need to be developed and I hope that this publication inspires further research from which evidence based interventions can be created.

My continuing interest in prevention spans over 30 years. It started with one of my earlier jobs in London's deprived inner city area, when I saw what a potently powerful and positive impact projects such as a Truancy School (where youngsters were only allowed to attend if they truanted over 90% from the school they were usually expected to attend), in which emotional literacy was propagated, had on youngsters with challenging behaviour.

I have witnessed hundreds and possibly thousands of individuals 'heal' and grow more robust as they engaged themselves with activities facilitating emotional wellness. I have witnessed feelings of emptiness and longing be replaced by ones of love and belonging, emotional hardship faced courageously and destructive energies turn into creative behaviours. Being involved with children and teenagers is exciting!

Anyone working with youngsters owes it to them, to work as well as they can, bearing in mind the budget and other available resources. This book contains much material, in terms of text and illustrations, to help smooth the path of the facilitator who is enabling emotional literacy in young people. It is aimed at teachers, psychologists and other related professionals. Developing emotional literacy can facilitate not only young people's good mental health but also their physical well-being, since the two are inextricably enmeshed. *Talking is for All* explains the theory behind emotional literacy, brings research findings together into one volume and offers tools for inexperienced and experienced facilitators to make emotional literacy an attainable goal.

Betty Rudd

About the author

Dr Betty Rudd, mother of four, is married and lives in Sussex. She qualified as a Specialist Teacher in the 1970s and as a Chartered Counselling Psychologist in the 1990s. Betty has over thirty years teaching experience ranging from pre-school children to adults. Originally trained as an actress at the Guildhall School of Music and Drama in the 1960s, she gained her PhD for her international research in psychology, from City University in 2000. She was one of the original members of the group who brought Circle Time from the USA to the UK and has been actively involved in the field ever since. There are currently seven books and twenty-one games that she has had published, mostly on emotional literacy, with others in the pipeline. The British Psychological Society name her as an expert in emotional literacy and body language, and she is therefore a frequent spokesperson on these issues. A co-founder of the Barnet Theatre-in-Education Team in London and the Forest Row Youth Centre in Sussex, a co-director of Two's Company Theatre and Hygeia Health Ltd., Betty is listed in 'Who's Who in the World'.

Introduction and structural overview

Welcome to *Talking is for All*, which is the second edition of the *Talking is…* trilogy and is a work in its own right.

Changes and additions in this edition

Updated research citations and the most recent references at the time of writing are within this second edition. I have expanded the teens' section to include teenagers up to 19 years. A new format dealing with research, theory, how to use the resources and a new section on resilience, substantially improves this edition when compared to the first one. A section listing useful resources is included after the references and an index for making navigation within the book simpler for readers, is added.

Prefaces or Forewords to previous editions are merged and expanded into a single preface for this one. After the Introduction, there is a section on Emotional Literacy, bringing together in one volume, research and theory on the topic. Worksheets show how to put it into practice. Emotional intelligence, which depends on emotional literacy, is part of seven multiple intelligences, that the psychologist Dr Howard Gardner (1993) thought of.

1 Linguistic (relating to words and languages)
2 Logical-Mathematical (relating to logic and arithmetic)
3 Musical (relating to sounds and rhythm)
4 Bodily-Kinesthetic (relating to controlling the movement of the body)
5 Spatial-Visual (relating to space and images)
6 Interpersonal (relating to others)
7 Intrapersonal (relating to self).

The term Emotional Intelligence is part of Interpersonal Intelligence which was expanded on from Howard Gardner's 'interpersonal' concept, by academics Mayer and Salovey (1993).

Talking is for All's structure

This edition is divided into three main parts. Firstly, four to seven year olds are dealt with, secondly, there is a part focusing on eight to twelves, and finally, the part which relates to the teenage years.

Features

Features include age-related stories, and exercises in the form of activities and worksheets.

Outline

The above features are within the book's outline of three main sections which embrace the following nine facets (though not necessarily in the same order).

1 Emotional literacy
2 Why emotional literacy is good
3 Who says what about emotions
4 New research
5 How to use the worksheets
6 Stories, activities and worksheets
7 Plans for using the stories
8 Worksheets
9 Resilience.

There are more interactive ideas in this book than in the three first editions. Some of these are dramatic – incorporating music, movement, art and drama as ways to develop emotional literacy across the curriculum. I think this is exciting. Just as in the first editions, the book is very accessible and easy to use.

CD Rom

The CD Rom contains PDF files of all the resources contained in Parts 1, 2 and 3. The CD contents are listed on pp.vi-viii of this book.

Emotional literacy overview

Emotional literacy is the ebb and flow of emotions linking thoughts and actions. The more emotionally literate people are, the higher their emotional intelligence. Emotional intelligence can be raised by teaching the five pillars of emotional literacy (Goleman, 1996 and Gottman, 1998):

1 Understand emotions in-the-moment. This is basic for self-knowledge and insight. The reason is that individuals who know their emotions are better at designing their journey through life, since they have a more certain sense of themselves, whom they like to be with and how they would like to spend their time.
2 Deal appropriately with emotions as they arise, such as shaking off irritability and gloom. This is fundamental for self-care. Individuals who are inept at managing their emotions, experience more distress, while people who are adept at it, bounce back quicker from negative stresses.
3 Have self-motivation. This is crucial for controlling emotions and delaying gratification in order to be attentive, creative and become a highly skilled person. Those with this ability tend to be more productive and create an effective impact with regard to anything they do.
4 Recognise emotions that others feel. For altruism and empathy fuelled by compassion, this is another basic principle. It is the individuals who have empathy that are the ones more likely to be in-tune with what others want and need.
5 Cope successfully with relationships. Being able to handle relationships is crucial because it involves coping with others' emotions; this is underpinned by qualities of effectiveness, popularity and leadership. Individuals who cope well with interpersonal relationships outshine others, than those who do not, when interacting.

Aspects of emotional literacy

Key aspects of emotional literacy include affect (emotion), behaviour (action) and cognition (thought) (Mortimer, 1998). Effective programmes include all these (Grant, 1992):

Affect

- Identify and name emotions
- Express emotions
- Assess level of emotions

- Manage emotions
- Delay gratification
- Control impulses
- Reduce stress
- Know that behaviour is not the same as emotion.

Behaviour

- Verbal: such as asking clearly for what one wants, reacting adequately to being criticised, standing up for oneself, being altruistic, listening non-judgementally to others and being involved in a positive peer group
- Non-verbal: having the skills to communicate effectively through body-language, gesturing, facial expression and eye contact.

Cognition

- Talking to oneself as a way of coping
- Being aware of one's environment and seeing oneself as part of that environment
- Having the skills to problem-solve such as finding alternative perspectives and anticipating outcomes
- Understanding others' viewpoints
- Knowing what behaviour is proper and what is not
- Being positive
- Becoming more aware of oneself.

Empathy, congruence and unconditional positive regard

The foundation within which an emotional literacy programme must be based is the communication, from teacher or therapist to youngster, of empathy (compassion), congruence (honesty) and unconditional positive regard (warm acceptance). There is cumulative research-based and clinical evidence showing that these three qualities are necessary for movement in a positive direction (Rogers, 1951; Rogers, 1961, Kirscherbaum and Henderson, 1989; Howe, 1993, Bayne et al, 1994 and Goleman, 2004).

Characteristics of emotionally literate individuals

Writers such as Apter (1997), Baker (1997), Goleman (1995), Gottman (1998), Rudd (1998 and 2001) and Schilling (1999) suggest that, emotionally literate people (when compared to those who are not) tend to show the following characteristics

- More confident
- Mentally healthier
- Less susceptible to ill health
- Quicker to recover from illness
- Skilled at coping with their emotions
- Able to recognise others'emotions
- Able to respond appropriately to others' emotions
- Happier
- More successful in relationships
- More successful in their careers
- Able to say 'No' to inappropriate situations
- Open to being educated
- Able to handle stress
- Able to resolve conflicts
- Good communicators
- Resilient in their self-esteem
- Aware of the environment
- Supportive of others in distress
- Good at communicating
- Able to understand another's point of view
- Have leadership qualities.

These qualities are coupled with confidence which shows behaviourally, while positively impacting on cognitive processes; for example, they think more clearly and speak up for themselves (Seligman, 2005). They are less likely to bully or to bully others (Gerhardt, 2004).

Vital role of class teacher

Teachers are in the favourable position of being able to make a special connection with their pupils, for facilitating emotional literacy, while linking valid theory with good teaching practice. Although there is an increasing body of literature supporting the premise that a positive mental attitude improves physical well-being, what is also needed is an overall and widely available practical framework, empirically based, which guides teachers in facilitating the improvement of emotional health in every pupil. A programme of emotional literacy within the school curriculum can give teachers a tool for working towards better class management while fostering positive behaviour in their pupils. (Such a programme is contained in the stories, activities and worksheets of this volume.)

Teachers may be the first to spot that a youngster is going through change, perhaps by noticing a behavioural difference. Relevant issues can be addressed during Circle Time so that youngsters are legitimately supported by others (Bliss et al, 1995). Fortunately, it is relatively easy for a network of peer support to be facilitated by teachers for their pupils. For example, each child or teenager could have a pupil who may be the same age or chronologically older, as a stress-buster-buddy to share emotions and concerns, mainly through talking. At the heart of such a relationship, it is vital to acknowledge the distress experienced (which can manifest physically) and give unconditional love (Batmanghelidijh, 2007).

Emotional and physical are enmeshed

Cumulative evidence shows that mental and physical aspects within people are entwined (Goleman, 1996; Grant, 1992; Baker, 1998 and Rudd, 2003). People without a supportive social network, who feel anxious and unhappy, are four times more likely to die significantly younger than those who have a social support network, a positive attitude and are emotionally literate (Baker, 1998). It is therefore considered paramount that teachers foster emotional literacy in their pupils as soon as they start school, until they leave. The most effective way of being psychologically healthy, is to be more expressive and aware of oneself. Being expressive helps with feeling good about oneself. (Baker, 1998; Gottman, 1998; Seligman, 2005; Gerdhardt, 2007 and Batmanghelidjh, 2007).

Feeling good and being healthy are linked to high self-esteem. If self-esteem is low, then more time is spent putting other peoples' wishes first, so there is little time and energy left to plan for health enhancing activities such as nutritious eating and an exercise programme. In such circumstances, it is easy to lose sight of one's individual needs and undermine one's health, while self-esteem plummets. The amount of self awareness one has, the level of compassion one experiences, the level of self-control, the ability to manage anger, make decisions and listen, determines ones strength in emotional literacy.

Psychoneuroimmunology

Psychoneuroimmunology: the investigation of the links between the mind, the immune and nervous systems, is increasingly showing the interactions between these areas and it is unrealistic to separate the mind from the body (Chopra, 1993 and Gerhardt, 2007). A short stressor such as giving a speech or showing a piece of work to classmates may increase immunity, long term stress such as being bullied or the break up of a relationship, can have a detrimental effect on health (Baker, 1998). This is because the amount of stress hormones (for example, cortisol) being released over a long period of time, suppress the immune system and interfere with the body's ability to protect against infection and cancer. The antidote to such stress is relaxation and being happy.

Tears and laughter
Laughter and tears can help prevent illness. This is because tears release stress-chemicals which have previously accumulated during a stressful time, and laughter reduces the levels of stress hormones such as cortisol while boosting an immunity

antibody called immunoglobin-A (Gottman, 1998; Seligman, 2005 and Gerdhardt, 2007). Those who engage in on-going cultural activities such as going to the theatre, writing, dancing or visiting art galleries, tend to live longer than people who rarely do these types of activities (Baker, 1998). It is not difficult to instil a love for these activities in youngsters if their teachers enjoy them.

The emotional mind

Educational writer, Schilling (1996), explains that the amygdala within the brain is the centre of the emotional mind and that all information entering the brain is analysed via the amygdala for emotional value before going to the cerebral cortex for processing. 'Data leaving the amygdala carry an emotional charge, which, if sufficiently powerful, can override reasoned thinking and logic' (p. 4). She then describes the work of the neo-cortex.

Brain, logic and emotion

'The critical networks on which emotion and feeling rely include not only the limbic system (amygdala), but also the neocortex – specifically the prefrontal lobe ... This part of the emotional brain is able to control feelings in order to reappraise situations and deal with them more effectively. It functions like the control room for planning and organising actions toward a goal. When an emotion triggers, within moments the prefrontal lobes analyse possible actions and choose the best alternative' (p. 5). These activities take place in the brain, but are not usually within awareness. Although the rational part of one's mind makes logical connections, the emotional part of the mind takes its beliefs to be absolutely true (Gottman, 1998). That is why it may appear futile when attempting to reason with a person who is emotionally distraught.

Sleep and arousal

The 'template' with which humans are born requires language and emotional instincts. Emotional instincts are so strong that if instinctive emotional reactions are inhibited daily, the need for emotional expression does not go away because one is in the cycle of emotional arousal. Griffin's (2001) research, as a psychologist, shows that an opportunity is therefore sought to complete the cycle of emotional arousal by rapid eye movement during the REM sleep phase.

He offers an explanation that links IQ level with emotion: the more emotionally aroused one is, the more IQ drops. Griffin explains that the amygdala stores and possesses the human survival templates as well as storing negative emotions. The thalamus puts the patterns of emotions together and flashes this information to the amygdala. Next, the amygdala gives emotional feeling to the information coming into it and therefore, emotions precede thoughts because emotion is present before it reaches the neo-cortex. His conclusion is that emotion triggers thought.

This view shows that if we are locked in a frame of reference that is distressing, we need to calm down and show a more effective way of connecting to reality. Griffin draws upon the role of imagination in the generation of desired goals and in solving psychological problems. It therefore follows that if we access our imagination we can imagine our future, plan and be creative. In emotional disorders the imagination is abused, so depressed individuals have negative fantasies, not positive ones. Anger is linked to depression, imagining violating the self and or other(s).

Anger

Inappropriately dealt with emotions, particularly anger, can have devastating effects – a research team offered a crucial piece of information regarding people with stress-related illnesses such as heart disease (Rudd, 2005a). Members of the team asked participants what specific personality characteristic causes illness? Each one of the researchers discovered identical answers: anger. This backs up the work of Chopra (1993) who also found that emotional attitude is connected to health related problems such as heart attacks. Chopra's investigations highlight that bottled-up anger, being depressed, stressed and emotionally reserved, are all associated with heart disease.

Decrease disruptive behaviour

Therefore, for improved emotional literacy, those who are behaviourally challenged can decrease their disruptive behaviour by learning anger management (Rudd, 2005a). For instance, one anger management technique is to put yourself in the other person's shoes as well as being aware of how you are emotionally and physically. Young people, as long as they are old enough to talk, can be guided in doing this within role-play situations. Intriguingly, in a three-year follow-up investigation, group members who trained in anger management reduced their drug and alcohol consumption while self-esteem increased (Rudd, 2005a).

Tolerate differences

What is imperative is the ability to tolerate differences in others while accepting them as they are. It is also helpful if individuals know their patterns of dealing with anger. Such knowledge may help them in being open to understanding that they have a variety of choices regarding how to cope with it (Rudd, 2005a). Inappropriately managed anger produces negative stress (Rudd, 2005b). Young people do not want negative stress, they want love. Research backs this up (McGrellis et al, 1998).

What young people hope

Reciprocal love is linked to emotional health. Research conducted by psychologist McGrellis and his team, spotlights that reciprocal love and material security are what young people hope for. They fear loneliness, illness, unemployment and homelessness. McGrellis and his team are not the only ones who have conducted research among school-aged individuals resulting in findings that these hopes and fears are common for young people in Britain (Swallow and Romick, 1998). Psychologists Swallow and Romick's research findings also reveal that young people need a sense of control about their future. Other research shows that youngsters feel insecure due to a sense of vulnerability and uncertainty (Nilson, 1998). Developing emotional literacy can help such youngsters gain a sense of control.

Lack of education

If a fraction of the money spent on treating physical illnesses was directed into emotional literacy education, a massive amount of suffering and of the UK's wealth could be saved. The cost of common mental disorders in England is at least £6 billion a year. Two-thirds of the British work-force is off work at some time, mainly due to anxiety or depression, of whom only ten per cent are referred to a specialist, as the capacity to cater for the other ninety per cent is not available. A great intervention move is needed to help individuals from undue suffering (Brown, 1998). Teachers can be key in implementing such a move.

Psychologist Martin (1998) offers a convincing argument for a new kind of relationship between youngster and school – one which is based on valuing good inter-personal relationships, so that a youngster does not experience school as a mainly lonely place. A curriculum embracing emotional literacy can achieve such a relationship. Meanwhile, psychologists Makin and Ruitenbeck (1998) state the importance of being in touch with your own psyche and to be active in promoting your health in order to be a good enough role model for the youngsters as they develop.

What schools can do

Since a young person spends many hours a day at school, there is much that can be done which can help towards re-dressing a possible shaky start to life, in terms of emotional wellness. For instance, a youngster may start school with low self-esteem due to perhaps an initial insecure attachment bond with the parent or primary care-giver; but school can become a stabilising factor in a child's life and if an adequate emotional literacy curriculum is followed throughout the early school years, by the time a child is between the ages of eight and twelve, it is not unusual to see some improvement in a desired direction in that child's emotional well being coupled with a rise in self-esteem and a marked improvement by age 18 (Perry, 2006). Many find their schooling difficult and some become disaffected with schools. Dealing with emotions is important for pupils not only because academic learning tends to become more enjoyable but because those with youngsters in their care will find that their job is easier when they have a group of emotionally literate youngsters (Rae, 2000).

Reduced mental suffering

If individuals were more emotionally literate, then the mental suffering, which has reached such large proportions in the UK, could be greatly reduced. Teachers are in an ideal position to teach emotional literacy, not only by talking but by ensuring communication. The way we communicate with youngsters profoundly influences their emotional development and way of relating. Communicate with awareness (Douglas, 2007). This psychological approach can create a learning environment that encourages and supports good behaviour (James and Brownsword, 1994).

Perspectives on emotional literacy

Emotional literacy is a controversial area and not all have been in favour of it; for example, according to Berne (1964), the creator of Transactional Analysis, people are better off thinking than feeling. However, his view was speculative, as opposed to being based on research. Steiner (1996), an old teacher of mine and a student of Berne who eventually worked with him, developed the view that being intelligent with emotions was wholesome. Steiner draws upon the research of others to argue his point, 'The possibility of monitoring minute facial muscle movements, respiration, perspiration, heat rate, brain activity, and other correlates of emotion has resulted in a great deal 0f research being reported ... Still ... emotional research in the *American Psychologist* offer little usable information' (National Advisory Mental Health Council, 1995, p. 32).

Shortly before Steiner's publication, Goleman (1995) offered a rational argument for emotional intelligence, saying that EQ was important because it relates to health, family life, work, emotional wellness and how well one does in life. So, although not all psychologists took the significance of emotions on board (Berne, 1970), others encompassed the importance of emotion in their work (Cassius, 1973; Jacobs, 1973; James, 1981 and Rudd, 2003). Psychologist Seligman (2005) also spotlights the importance of emotion, focusing on the good effects of positive emotions.

Psychologists share research findings

Psychologists Griffin and Tyrrell (2001) share findings, from research conducted at Delaware University, that emotional knowledge is a predictor of social behaviour and academic competence in youngsters at risk. Evidence from this research shows that young people who come from disadvantaged backgrounds but who can read the emotional facial expressions of other people, are more likely to integrate socially and be academically successful when compared to those from disadvantaged homes who cannot understand the facial expressions of emotions other people experience.

IQ and EQ

Traditionally, rational skills are measured by IQ tests and tend to be prioritized within the state educational system. EQ, however, is at least as important. A reason for this is that both rational and emotional skills are inter-linked within overall human intelligence. If rational intelligence is better with higher emotional intelligence and emotional intelligence benefits from the rational mind, then the two forms of intelligence work best together and are interdependent (Schilling, 1999).

Games

As psychotherapists, psychologists, counsellors and/or educators, we have a responsibility to facilitate developing emotional literacy within the young people in our care. What seems most important is that we do it. Perhaps not so important, is how we do it. One way of doing it, apart from using this book, is to utilize games that facilitate raising EQ (Rudd, 2002).

Games that foster emotional literacy can have positive outcomes. From personal experience, I know these types of self-disclosing activities have benefits such as learning to listen with quality attention (which creates rapport), to collaborate (which brings about interaction), to have fun (which has the benefit of boosting the immune system), to discover something new about self and others (which keeps the brain healthily active), to deepen relationships (which facilitates a sense of love), to be a member of a co-operative group (which enables a feeling of belonging) and to be positively interactive (which aids communication skills).

Government's influence

Whatever programme of literacies or intelligences schools propagate, is partly dependent on government. During the Thatcher era in Britain, the more pupils schools had, the more money the government gave them. Success was measured by the school's league tables (Sassoon, 2001). Consequently, youngsters with emotional and behavioural disorder (EBD) were not welcomed in schools, since the time and attention they needed, could be offered to more young people without EBD. There was less time available in schools for developing emotional literacy, since the time was needed to focus on numeracy and literacy for the league tables. Due to this, the number of young people permanently excluded from schools rose by approximately 10,000 between 1990/1 and 1996/7, from 2,910 to 12,700 (Rasmussen, 2001).

At the time of writing, the British government directed schools to work closely with parents of youngsters at risk of expulsion, by having a pastoral system. Due to this plan, the number of young people who have been expelled from schools has fallen from 12,700 to 8,600 within four years. Nevertheless, the UK National Curriculum has its limitations and although Citizenship sessions have been compulsory in secondary schools since September 2002, it is not easy for primary schools to find time, in an apparently overcrowded curriculum, for nurturing children's personal, social and health education (PSHE); although there is an aspiration for regular Circle Time sessions where children can specifically work on increasing their emotional literacy.

Support

To achieve a generation of emotionally literate youngsters, support is needed from parents and government initiatives. I have had the privilege to supervise several psychologists who work for UK's A Place to Be. This initiative is run as a charity that focuses on primary schools. A therapist with an educational background works with youngsters who suffer from emotional problems identified by the school. The service is only available in some schools and only those whose needs are perceived as the greatest are offered support, due to restriction in funds. It seems likely that every school can benefit from a similar initiative and other like-minded projects. For example, parenting classes, an outreach staff member who can investigate why a young person has started to truant, specialist teachers in art, music, dance and drama (especially for those who underachieve), the supply of nutritional meals and counselling services. However, unless resources such as finances are made available, youngsters can lose out by not fulfilling their potential for using their emotions intelligently. 'Emotional intelligence' is almost a household term, this has not always been the case.

Reviewing emotional literacy

Two relatively unknown academic psychologists, Mayer and Salovey (1993), had a paper published in an obscure professional journal, which was less than ten pages long, called 'The Intelligence of Emotional Intelligence'. Less than a decade later, a plethora of literature accumulated , mostly speculative, stemming from their work.

Emotional intelligence

Two years after Mayer and Salovey's paper, Goleman (1995) published 'Emotional Intelligence', declaring that the times we live in now are in need of compassion and self-restraint. He showed that neurological information implies that there is an opportunity for changing the emotional habits. Goleman does this by explaining that we are born with the neurological tools for experiencing emotion. Therefore, we may learn to control emotion, be empathic and cope with relationships. The way we handle emotion is key in either maintaining treasured relationships or ruining them. It is also key to our well being and how we cope.

The brain's plasticity

As early as 1975, Goleman persuasively argued that our emotional heritage is the basis of temperament, but that temperament is not destiny, since our brain chemistry has remarkable plasticity. The way we learn how to cope with emotions as a child, lays the path for how inept or adept we become in handling emotions as an adult. The critical periods for putting down the critical emotional habits that will rule our lives are during the developmental years. These habits, however, can be modified later in life.

Over 20 years after Goleman's publication, Steiner (1997) declared the same sentiment, using different phraseology. In the same vein, Schilling (1999) and Weisinger (1998) state in their writings that during a young person's development it is necessary to address emotional literacy. Gerhardt (2004) and Batmanghelidijh (2007) also write similarly, although Gerhardt bases her work on scientific research while Batmanghelidijh bases hers on evidence from her work as a child psychotherapist. With people who have such authority all agreeing with one another, it seems obvious that it can never be too late to improve emotional literacy, or too early to facilitate it.

Born emotional

We are born emotional beings. Ancient Greeks knew this. Early Greek philosopher Aristotle declared, 'The greatest thing by far is to have a command of emotion'. In the 21st century, psychologist Mair (2001) stated that emotions are more crucial than thinking. He stipulates that feelings are important in therapy work. Similarly, I declare that they are important for teaching and other work which involves adult to teenager and or child interaction.

Value emotions

Mair values emotions and does not want them ignored. Likewise, Griffin (2001) says that we need to pay attention to emotions. He explains how one can be eloquent in speech yet emotionally locked up. Young people need to learn to express feelings in words because if they do not learn this skill it is much harder to keep adult relationships healthy. There is pressure on youngsters to survive academically yet what is also needed for them is emotional support to develop emotional literacy.

In Britain

According to the Chief Executive of the British Mental Health Foundation, Ruth Lesirge, at least one in five children in Britain suffer from psychological problems (Lesirge, 2001a/b). Although literacy and numeracy are important, if youngsters could also be taught social skills and how to effectively deal with emotions, then there could be less mental distress later in their lives. Lesirge investigates the impact of certain types of support in schools where there are young people who are behaviourally challenging, have depression and experience isolation (2001a/b). The types of support embrace Circle Time, Friends Circles (other children volunteer to be special friends to a child who is either isolated or withdrawn), parents room, parenting skills programme and training workshops for all staff (whether a lunch supervisor or a teacher).

These projects were based in certain mainstream schools in the UK (such as in Doncaster, Guildford, Coventry and Sheffield) and the outcomes show that they are effective with youngsters for promoting their confidence, self-esteem and positive mental health.

Involve parents

Such news is heart-warming. However, educational consultant with Schools Support Services in Britain, Sassoon (2001), claims that schools alone cannot help develop youngsters' emotional literacy. His view is that parents, too, should be involved.

Perpetrators are also victims

Sassoon is not the first to declare that perpetrators are also victims. Morrison (1997) offers a convincing argument that young perpetrators are also victims, exemplified by his graphical description of the home circumstances of Jon Venables and Robert Thompson who were convicted of murder.

Money

If the £130,000 (or even just fraction of it) of tax payers money spent per year on Venables and Thompson for their care and education while they were incarcerated had been available prior to the Bulger tragedy to invest into the Venables and Thompson families, and the two boys, in order to help them in coping with life, James Bulger would probably be alive now (Sassoon, 2001). It is important to hear what professionals such as Sassoon and Morrison say to other professionals regarding youngsters' well-being.

Professional audience

For a professional audience, who says what regarding emotional literacy in children and teenagers, can be divided into three main areas:

1 Professionals journals such as *Young Children* and *Young Exceptional Children* (these offer a combination of the scientific basis offered by researchers on enriching emotional literacy and practical information on how to develop it in young individuals).
2 Specific practical information on teaching the young how to identify, understand and express emotions healthily (for example Joseph and Strain, 2003a; Joseph and Strain, 2003b; Kusche and Greenberg, 1994; Shure, 2000; Webster-Stratton, 1990 and Webster-Stratton, 1999).
3 Researchers who have had their findings published, with regard to the effects of enhancing emotional literacy in young people (for example Denham and Burton, 1996; Domitrovich et al, 2002; Greenberg and Kursche, 1998; Moore and Beland, 1992 and Webster-Sutton and Hammonds, 1997).

Below are deliberations on the implications of investigations such as these.

More emotional literacy, less truancy

What we know from researchers such as these is revealing. For instance, there are statistically significant differences between the numbers of young people who truant from schools and the availability of emotional literacy programmes – the main factor is that schools which offer emotional literacy programmes have the least truants and exclusions. This is exemplified by Holland Park School in West London, where Andrea Atkinson heads a project on social inclusion. She works closely with heads of departments, two youth workers, a learning support co-ordinator and two learning support mentors in order to provide a comprehensive support programme; a member of staff from the local social services department is also assigned to work at the school. Due to this strategy, fixed term exclusions at the school dropped by 75 per cent and within two years, permanent exclusions were reduced by 65 per cent (Sassoon, 2001). The amount of stress relieved by emotional literacy programmes is priceless.

Stress

Ability to develop insight into stressors is important. Emotions, thoughts and beliefs can make stress either negative or positive. If, for instance, a child is told to play hide and seek and that child loves the game, then it is a good stressor; but if the child hates that game, then it is a bad stressor. In order to help youngsters develop stress coping skills, it is essential to develop the ability to manage stress within you, the adult. Stress which creates motivation and creativity is positive stress. Resilience buffers against negative stress while allowing positive stress.

Resilience

Professional helpers such as psychotherapists and teachers are faced with the needs of others, practically, daily and often for many years; so mental resilience is important. In order to stay psychologically robustly healthy, the following ideas, which have mainly been extrapolated from Baker (1998) and Rudd (2006), can be used as a framework for an antidote to negative stress, so the ability to handle pupils and clients does not impinge on the helpers' psychological wellness. Relax, be happy, use spontaneity, have a positive attitude, do some cultural activities (as some people who live longer than average do, such as going to the theatre, visiting art galleries and writing), eat nutritiously, drink enough water, exercise regularly, keep your own needs in sight, recognise and deal with your own feelings. In sum, take adequate self-care.

Conclusion

Youngsters need wise and loving caretakers, nutrition, rest and play as they develop. Play to a child is like work to an adult. It is important because a whole plethora of emotions can be safely expressed during play.

Pre-school children need to experience playing with their bodies, such as playing finger games, in order to gain in self-awareness (Brooking-Payne, 1996). Self-awareness is crucial for emotional literacy. The years from four to nineteen (and beyond), are an exciting time of change from a young child to a young adult and boundaries are needed so that youngsters can test their strength against them, while feeling secure and being reassured. Teenagers continue to need acceptance and unconditional love no less than nutritious food and drink since all these types of support are nurturing. Indeed, educational writer Brooking-Payne believes that Circle Time activities (which incorporates emotional literacy education) need to be continued at least up to the age of 21, for the optimum development of young people.

I am moved to declare with my heart and mind that what emerges from emotional development can be extraordinarily and profoundly positive for the individual, society and the world. The younger generation inherits what we have made of the world, those with good emotional intelligence will keep this world, including themselves, OK. If they do not and they are emotionally intelligent, they will feel uncomfortable and so will then do something about it. Further, they will have the ability to be healthier, more well adjusted and happier than if they had not been nurtured to have psychological well being.

You, the adults involved, are invaluable. See the beauty inherent in every young person and relate to them with loving wisdom (such as patience) as you facilitate their emotional literacy. Your non-verbal communication whilst being with them, such as your behaviour, attitude and vocal quality, speaks statistically significantly louder than words (Rudd, 2000). Developing emotional literacy in youngsters is not difficult. Why are you taking young people on this emotional literacy educational journey? Perhaps because it is fundamental that youngsters feel confident and secure within themselves, that they learn to listen to their own needs and be respectful of others, that they learn how to learn, that they are social and healthy not only today but for life.

How to use the resources

Worksheets and activities in this book are rooted in the theory and research based evidence of experts in the field of emotional literacy (such as Goleman, 2004 and Steiner, 1980). Creative interpersonal and intra-personal activities are combined with learning about emotional wellness, sharing, talking, thinking, feeling and doing.

Teachers can use the resoures in a step-by-step way, to teach emotional literacy by planning, implementing, assessing and record-keeping a quality curriculum. Psychological practitioners can integrate appropriate worksheets into whatever therapeutic model they use with a particular child, teenager or group. Worksheets are self explanatory and can also be used to keep youngsters creatively occupied while in a waiting room or whilst following up an activity.

Adapt suggested activities

Each activity sheet contributes to an emotional literacy programme. The programme is flexible so you can use your own creativity, and the imagination of the children and teenagers. Use the suggested activities as they are or adapt them so that they are tailor-made for your particular child, teenager or group.

Planning

When planning for your youngster(s), bear in mind the following two points.

1 Ensure that the five pillars of the emotional literacy programme or curriculum are covered (know your emotions, manage them, recognise others' emotions, motivate yourself and handle relationships well). This can be done by having the list in front of you and or ticking each one off as you introduce it.
2 Ensure that there is a link with parents and carers so they know what is happening. You can do this, for example, by either giving appropriate homework, or via a newsletter. If possible, invite parents and carers to attend a meeting about the emotional literacy curriculum. In this way they will be able to support it.

Collect evidence

Keep every scrap of evidence to support your emotional literacy programme. At an appropriate time, display all the work and invite an audience so the youngsters can show their personal and combined achievements. When possible, take photographs, film and audio-record individuals and groups while working on emotional literacy. (This requires informed consent from young people, and their parents or carers if the youngsters are not legally adults.) The eventual bank of evidence can be useful for qualitative and quantitative research.

Record keeping

An age appropriate assessment form is in each of the relevant sections (Parts 1, 2 and 3) which can also be used for record keeping. These forms can easily be adapted to suit your particular situation. Each form takes less than five minutes to administrate. It is suggested that a record of assessment is obtained when you first have your group or youngster, half way through your time with the group or youngster, and when it is time for this group or youngster to move on. Children and teenagers can also record their own achievements while with you. They can do this by implementing their own record keeping.

Worksheets can be used either independently, or as part of a planned course. If you use the worksheets as part of a curriculum on emotional literacy, you may like to consider making a plan of what your aims are, such as, for a session, a week, a month, a term or on a yearly basis and or more.

Materials and resources

Ensure that all youngsters have access to colouring in equipment.
Parts 1, 2 and 3 embrace the materials and resources.

Part One

Talking is for Kids: Emotional literacy for 4–7 year olds

Introduction
Record keeping and assessment
Stories and activities
Plans for using the worksheets
Worksheets

Introduction

Within the four to seven year age range, expect children to build on what they have previously assimilated, to focus on relatively immediate goals such as wanting attention NOW. However, they are growing in their awareness of time and can be expected to predict future events, such as being at a birthday party. With the help of a facilitator, they are able to plan goals for the near future, such as making sandwiches in the morning and wrapping them up to stay fresh so they can have them at lunch or tea time. They normally smile when smiled at, laugh and cry with you; share willingly and offer comfort if another child is in distress. They should be able to identify their feelings of happiness, sadness and anger and know that it is OK to have different emotions.

Stories in this section are especially written with the aim of supporting four to seven year olds in their emotional literacy development. They can be used independently, although worksheets relate to them. Children aged four, five, six and seven also need to continue with familiar touching games such as clapping games, so that they gain a sense of security during a time of change, in order not to become 'emotionally dry' (Brooking-Payne, 1996, p. 22).

Record keeping and assessment

Record keeping is important because children, parents and facilitators can see, at a glance, what youngsters have covered. Similarly with assessments; it is easy to become aware of what level or stage a young person has reached. With this in mind, assessment and record forms are included before the stories. However, there is a further form which can be used simultaneously as a record and as a form of assessment, that can be filled in by the child (perhaps after discussion with a facilitator) on worksheet 19.

Assessment form (to be filled in by the facilitator)

Child's name: ....

Aspects and skills	1st date	2nd date	3rd date
Feels secure in setting			
Has sense of self-worth			
Is gaining confidence			
Orientates self in surroundings			
Respectful of others			
Feels she or he belongs			
Experiences achievement			
Expresses own needs and wants			
Listens without interrupting			
Is honest			
Has compassion			
Can turn-take			
Joins in group activity			
Plays or interacts with others fairly			
Copes with change			
Works alone for 15 minutes			

My record (to be filled in by the young person)

My name is ....

I worked on this sheet on (date) ....

It took me .... minutes to finish it.

I felt ... (write your feeling and or draw an appropriate face in the space below) doing it.

```



```

I am pleased/not pleased (delete appropriately and draw appropriate face in the space below) I did it.

```


```

I know how to follow rules: Yes/No (delete appropriately)

I have a friend called ....

I feel ....

I think that ....

What I want to do is ....

Stories and activities

Story 1
Jerry goes shopping

Jerry went shopping with his dad. He was six years old and it was two days before Nazmin's birthday party. His dad said, 'Let's go to the toy shop to buy your friend Nazmin a birthday present.' 'Oh! Yes! Hurrah!' Jerry shouted, jumping up and down with delight. They walked up a steep hill to the zebra crossing, crossed when it was safe and went through the toy shop doorway. This shop was full of things that Jerry wanted. He looked at everything, from the little bouncy balls to the big go-carts. Meanwhile, his dad found a present which he thought would be suitable for Nazmin.

'Do you think Nazmin would like this face painting set?' he asked. 'Mmmm.' Jerry nodded, and carried on looking around the toy shop. In the corner of the shop he saw a lady demonstrating a bendy toy and saying, 'Every child should have one.' The toy fascinated Jerry, especially the way it could be bent in any position. After hearing the lady repeat her statement, 'Every child should have one.' He picked up a bendy toy and put it in his pocket to take home.

His father paid for the face painting set, then Jerry and his dad happily walked back to their flat holding hands. When they had arrived at their flat, Jerry's dad took the face painting set out of the shopping bag and Jerry took the bendy toy out of his pocket. 'Where did you get that?' Dad shouted. Jerry looked scared, 'The shop. The lady said, "Every child should have one".' Jerry responded. 'You stole it! It doesn't belong to you does it? It must go back.' Jerry was very sorry that he had taken the toy and wanted to take it back to the shop. Then Jerry and his dad returned the bendy toy to the shop. Jerry cried, 'I'm sorry. I won't do it again.' Jerry's dad forgave him. Then they went home to wrap up Nazmin's present.

Follow-up questions and activities for 'Jerry goes shopping'

Aims social and moral development, problem-solving, learning to learn while becoming self-aware, being interactive, using movement, art and drama.

What did Jerry do that was wrong?
What should Jerry have done?
What would you like for a birthday present?

How would you feel if someone stole something from you?

Stand up and make up a simple movement that you can repeat three times, which shows how Jerry's dad felt when he realised that Jerry had stolen a toy.

Illustrate the story.

With a partner, make up a different ending for the story.

With your partner, paint a scene which shows the different ending.

Everyone can display their paintings.

Get into a group of three or four and make a short play of the story.

Worksheets 20 and 5 can be used with story 1.

Story 2
Monique and her kitten

Monique was four years old and her mother brought home a gorgeous fluffy little black and white kitten during the Easter school holiday. They called it Fluffy. Monique loved Fluffy. She fed, watered and stroked it daily. One morning, after breakfast, Monique wanted to play with her kitten. She called to it lovingly. She looked for it upstairs, downstairs and in the garden. She could not find it anywhere. Monique was so unhappy because she could not find Fluffy, that she started crying. Big sad tears rolled down her red little cheeks as she opened the front door.

Monique walked along the pavement outside her house crying, 'Fluffy Fluffy Fluffy!' When Monique's mother noticed that the front door was open, she realised that Monique had left the house. Monique's mother rushed outside to find her. She spotted her at the corner of the pavement holding Fluffy. Quickly, she ran to bring Monique and Fluffy back into the house.

Follow-up questions and activities for 'Monique and her kitten'

Aims Interaction, increase awareness, learn to learn, develop confidence, use art, drama and movement for problem solving.

How do you think Monique's mum felt when she saw that the front door was open?
What do you think that Monique should have done when she could not find Fluffy?
How would you feel if you could not find your favourite person?
Talk about this question with a partner: What do you think Monique's mother will say to her when they are back in the house?
Find a space and make a movement with your whole body, which you can repeat three times, that shows how you think Monique's mum felt when she found Monique.
Get into twos or threes and act out the story.
Make up a different ending to the story.
Illustrate the story.

Worksheets 21 and 7 can be used with story 2.

Story 3
Clever Thomas

Once upon a time a lovely little boy was born to two doting parents. His mother was Emma and his father, Aristoteles. Thomas grew up to be a tall and clever seven-year-old. Unfortunately, he did not like going to school because some children called him 'Fatty'. He kept this a secret, not telling anybody, so no one knew why he did not like going to school.

One morning, Thomas would not get out of bed to go to school. When his mum and dad pulled his bed-covers off him to get him up, he burst out crying and shouted, 'I hate school! I'm never gong to school!' His parents made him go. At school that day, he was very quiet and in the playground during a playtime break he picked on a small child and called him, 'Skinny'. Then he felt guilty at being mean to the small child so he quickly said, 'Sorry. I didn't mean it.'

Thomas was so miserable, that he did not eat his packed lunch but only had his drink. After school, when he was at home, he went straight to his room and cried because some people had called him 'Fatty' at school. That evening his mum and dad cuddled him and eventually he told them his problem.

Follow-up questions and activities for 'Clever Thomas'

Aims Express emotions, develop socially, increase self-awareness, problem-solve, learn how to learn, be empathic, process interpersonally, interact, use art and drama.

If a friend wants to play with you, how do you feel?
How do you think Thomas felt straight after he shared his problem with his mum and dad?
Make up the last bit of the story and finish with the words: 'they lived happily ever after.'
Imagine how you would feel if you were being bullied, then draw that feeling.
Draw or paint a different feeling to the one you drew above.
Find a partner to talk about this question: Have you bullied any person?
With your partner, see how many answers you can find between you, to the following question: What should his (Thomas') parents now do?
With your partner, talk about what makes each of you unhappy and happy.
Get into a group of four or five and act out the story.

Worksheets 22 and 1 can be used with story 3.

Story 4
Peter in the playground

There was snow in the playground and it was so cold that the children were allowed into their classrooms early. Peter was in the reception class and uncomfortable about not getting most of the attention; so he talked a lot. He did this to make others look at him. During one cold morning, the teacher told the reception class children, 'All of you, during the lunch-break, stay indoors, because it is freezing cold outside.' Peter was too busy talking to hear what his teacher, Mr. Michael, said, but all the other children heard him.

When it was lunch time, Peter put on his coat and went into the playground. No one else was there and his fingers were so cold that he found it hard to move them. A dinner-lady found him shivering, huddled in a corner of the playground. "Why aren't you in your classroom?" she asked. "We're not allowed in during lunch time." Peter explained. The dinner lady responded, "I know, but today your teacher said that you are allowed in. I'll take you to your teacher." When Peter was taken to his teacher, Mr. Michael explained why it was important for him to stop talking and listen sometimes.

Follow-up questions and activities for 'Peter in the playground'

Aims   problem-solve, learn to find things out for one's own self, environmental awareness, social development, emotional expression, move towards independence and build confidence.

When should have Peter stopped talking to listen?
How did Peter feel when he was alone in the playground?
How do you keep warm?
With a partner, role-play the situation for five minutes each way. One is Peter while the other finds Peter in the playground and communicates to him what he or she understands Peter's feelings to be.
Discuss how you would feel, what you would think and do, if you found Peter in the playground.
On your own, think of ways of clearing the ice and snow in the playground so it is not so cold and slippery under the feet, then share what you have thought of, with your partner.

Worksheet 2 can be used with story 4.

Story 5
Isabella had a friend

It was the long school summer holiday and Isabella was going move from Key Stage One to Key Stage Two in September (in the 'old days' she would have moved from Infants to the Juniors). She had a friend called Jilly. Isabella and Jilly were playing hide-and-seek with their childminder. While Isabella was hiding, she thought, 'Jilly's a long time finding me. I wonder if she's stopped looking for me? I'll go and find her and my childminder.' Neither Isabella nor her childminder could find Jilly.

Eventually, they heard her shouting, 'Look what Isabella's done to the car!' Isabella did not know what Jilly was talking about. Then she heard the childminder's cross voice, 'Isabella! You naughty girl! I don't like having you here if that's the kind of thing you're going to do! I'm telling your granny!' (Isabella lived with her grandmother.) Isabella gasped, 'What is it?' The childminder angrily pulled Isabella to the car which was parked in the garage. The word 'Isabella' had recently been scratched onto it, in secret, by Jilly. Isabella said, 'I didn't do it'. Jilly looked at the childminder, straight into her eyes and clearly said, 'Yes she did'. The childminder did not know whether to believe Jilly. Nevertheless, she telephoned Isabella's grandmother so that Isabella could be taken home early that day. The childminder also made arrangements for Jilly to go home early too. While waiting for her granny, Isabella insisted to the childminder that she did not scratch the car. Soon, both girls were taken to their respective homes.

Follow-up questions and activities for 'Isabella had a friend'

Aims   Build confidence, interact, be honest, creative, process intra-personally, learn to learn, social development, use music and drama.

How would you feel if you knew your friend could never lie to you?
What do you think should happen next in the story?
Is there any time when you would tell a lie?
What do you think of Jilly?
Find a partner and tell your partner of a time when someone upset you.
Get into a group of three or four and act out the story.
Within your group, discuss ways of dealing with Jilly's lie and Isabella's feelings.
Think about the type of music that is like Isabella's feelings and make sounds that remind you of her feelings. Each member of the group adds their own vocal sound in turn, until all group members make their sounds together, like an orchestra.

Worksheet 3 can be used with story 5.

Plans for using the worksheets

If there is no separate plan for using a worksheet, then the worksheet itself is self-explanatory.

Plans for using worksheets 1 to 18

Talking is for kids

Aim   For children to work towards appropriate inter-dependence and independence.

Either copy or print out the worksheets so that every child can put them in order to make up one comic each.

Children help one another to secure the ordered worksheets together into a booklet.

Read out the story in the worksheets, which can be followed by discussion. The children share colouring-in equipment to colour their booklets, with the option of taking them home to finish and show-off.

Plan for using worksheet 4

Talking isn't medicine

Aim   For children to know their emotions.

Invite children to move how they feel while you join in.

Invite children to make a sound, individually in turn and then altogether, which shows how they feel; in this way they are making human-music about their emotions.

Give children information by explaining how some people take medicines which can hide how they feel, and how healthy it is to know how you feel.

Invite children to talk to one another and to you, about how they feel; you may like to say how you feel yourself, to start this process going.

Hand out worksheet 4 for each child to colour in, on his or her own. Children can finish the activity in their own time.

Plan for using worksheet 6

You can feel bad if ...

Aim   Managing emotions.

Invite children to talk about their favourite animals.
Share about a time when you had a bereavement and how you got over it.
Explain that sometimes pets do not live as long as people and how we can look after animals while they are in our care; and how we can cope when they die, such as remembering happy memories of them.
Hand out worksheet 6 to colour in.

Plan for using worksheet 8

You can feel bad because ...

Aim   Self-motivation.

In small groups, each child describes a time they felt rather distressed yet persevered for the better, such as during a test, or not waking up parents at night due to knowing that there was nothing really wrong.
Ask the children for examples of when they can continue to do something, having a goal in mind; for instance, saving some pocket money for an expensive toy (they may come up with a surprising plethora of ideas during discussion).
Hand out worksheet 8 to colour in. Also draw one or more of the ideas which emerged from step 2 above (where their perseverance led to achievement).

Plan for using worksheet 9

You feeling good

Aim   Identify others' emotions.

(Bring in some happy-sounding music, such as a recording of Mozart's *Rondo a la Turk* to play for the children.)

Ask the children to think of two wishes each of them have, one of which is realistically possible and one impossible.
Ask the children to get into pairs and discuss how they can each make their possible wish come true.

Show a teddy bear and say that teddy's wish came true.
Say that teddy is smiling.
Ask the children to identify teddy's emotion.
Put on the happy sounding music e.g. Mozart's *Rondo a la Turk* for the children to listen to for a few minutes. Explain that this music reminds you of how teddy feels.
Hand out worksheet 9 to colour in; alternatively, the children can draw or paint either a teddy bear or a wish.

Plan for using worksheet 10

Five ways to feel good

Aim   Coping with relationships.

(You may like to ask each child to bring a teddy bear and a doll as well as any musical instrument that they can play, for the following activity.)

Show a teddy bear and explain that teddy is crying because his tower of bricks toppled down.
Say that along comes teddy's friend dolly who cuddles teddy.
Teddy and dolly build another tower.
Teddy and dolly have a picnic.
Teddy and dolly have a rest.
Ask the children to get into groups of approximately six. One of them can use a toy bear as a puppet, another can use a doll as a puppet and the remaining can take turns to be the narrator or narrate altogether (apart from children who will play musical instruments). Each group gives a 'puppet show' of the above scenario (steps 1 to 5) to the other groups; before and after each puppet show, a different child can play an instrument – as an 'interlude'.
Encourage the children to talk in groups about who they like to spend their time with.
Children brainstorm different ways of making up with a friend they have broken up with.
Children brainstorm ways of being healthy and taking care of themselves.
Hand out worksheet 10 to colour in.

Plan for using worksheet 11

Healthy mind and body

Aim   Learning to learn.

Ask the children what would happen if they did not have any water for a very long time.

Explain what a desert and oasis are.

Tell them to close their eyes and imagine what it feels like to be thirsty then ask them to move around (they can open their eyes for this part) as if they are walking in a desert very thirsty; inform them that when you clap your hands, they see an oasis.

Discuss feelings before, during and after seeing the oasis.

Ask the children what they feel if they do not have enough to drink.

Tell the children to get into small groups of approximately four and ask them to talk about what would happen if they did not eat for a very long time. After a few minutes, ask for feedback from each group.

Ask the children what they feel when they do not have enough to eat.

Ask the children what they should do when they are thirsty.

Ask the children what they should do when they are hungry.

Hand out worksheet 11 to colour in and or ask each child to draw a picture of a person in a desert at an oasis which they can colour in if they wish.

Plan for using worksheet 12

Grow strong and healthy

Aim   Independence.

(Any child who knows how to play a musical instrument can bring it. Alternatively, hand out percussion instruments or make them.)

Draw a seed.
Draw roots on the seed.
Make the above into a seedling.
Change the seedling into a flower.
Think of what was needed so that the seed could grow into a strong and healthy flower.
Find a partner and share your ideas about what seeds need to develop into flowers.
Get into groups of four to six people to act our growing from seeds into flowers (for example, a few people can be seeds growing into flowers, others can be the sun and the rain).
Join with another group, one of the groups does the acting while the other group adds music to the action. Each group performs to the others, in turn.
As a whole group, talk about everything you need to grow strong and healthy.
Colour in worksheet 12.

Plan for using worksheet 13

Play with friends

Aim   Being social.

In a circle, helper whispers either 'duck', 'cow' or 'pig' to each child.
With eyes closed, children make either 'quack', 'moo' or 'oink' sounds,
around until they are in three groups; a group of ducks, one of cows and
another of pigs.
Each group make up a play lasting about two minutes, about a visitor who
comes to stay in our world from a different world, so the guest needs to be
taught how to be polite and well-mannered.
Each group shows their mini-play to the other groups.
Hand out worksheet 13 to colour in.

Plan for using worksheet 14

Grow and heal

Aim   Environmental awareness.

On you own, think about a dirty and untidy room.
With a partner, talk about how to make a dirty and untidy room, clean and tidy.
Discuss the importance of caring for our environment.
Think about getting enough sleep and why we need it.
Draw a picture of what you think that you would like to do if you were
feeling tired after working hard at cleaning and tidying up.
Stick the picture on the wall for everyone to see. You can also write about it
if you wish, and perhaps read out one of your phrases or sentences.
Colour in worksheet 14.

Plan for using worksheet 15

Be happy

Aim   Happiness.

Talk about the importance of feeling fine about yourself so that you can be
happy.
With a partner, think about the things that make you happy.

In groups, write and draw all the things that make you happy.
Each group share what makes them happy.
Each child decides what they will do to be happy.
Colour in worksheet 15.

Plan for using worksheet 16

Your feelings

Aim   Express feelings.

(Rule: Do not touch anyone or anything and stay in your 'corner' while shouting. First, the helper can demonstrate the following three-cornered drama game or exercise.)

Three children stand at three points of an invisible triangle. One corner is called 'the love corner', the other is called 'the need corner' and the third is called 'the hate corner'.

At a given signal the three children simultaneously shout 'I love you', 'I need you' and 'I hate you', respectively, for approximately ten seconds. Then in a clockwise direction they change places, then after another ten seconds of shouting their different word they change places again, so after about 30 seconds, each child has had a turn expressing need, hate and love.

Do this until all children have had a turn.

Discuss how each child felt doing the above and say that this is a warm up used by some actors, since they need to be able to express emotions safely.

Hand out worksheet 16 to colour in.

Plan for using worksheet 17

Balance your life

Aim   To gain confidence.

(Rule: Freeze at a given signal and continue at another given signal.)

The children each simultaneously mime what they do from getting up in the morning to sleeping at night.

At various times throughout the miming, ask the children to freeze in their positions apart from one or two children, who watch the rest for a few moments, before all continue with their mimes again.

As in step 2 until all the children have had the opportunity to show some of their mime to the others.

In small groups, discuss the importance of a balanced life. For example, if you do not eat anything except sweets you will get too fat, develop spots and lose some teeth.

Each group eventually shares their ideas with everyone.

Hand out worksheet 17 to colour in.

Plan for using worksheet 18

Be kind to yourself

Aim   Keep sight of your own needs.

(Rule: When pretending to be a sleeping lion, youngsters do not move or make a sound.)

Find a space and pretend to be a sleeping lion.

Listen to sounds outside the building you are in.

Listen to sounds outside the room you are in.

Listen to sounds inside the room you are in.

Listen to yourself, such as your breathing and heartbeat. How do you feel doing this?

Think of all that you need to keep yourself happy and healthy, and imagine giving yourself all that you need whenever you need it.

Colour in worksheet 18.

Plan for using worksheet 23

Feel secure in setting

Aim   For children to feel secure in their setting.

Escort your group of children on a guided tour around the immediate vicinity showing them the following. The games area outside the room and inside the room you use, the work area inside and outside the room, the emotional literacy session area, the cloakroom, where the tissues are kept for runny noses, the waste paper bin, the toilet and wash basin.

In pairs (one of the pair is named Apple and the other is Pear). Apples show pears: a) the games, work and session areas; b) the wash basin; c) where the tissues are kept. Then the Pears show the Apples: a) the cloakroom; b) the waste paper basket; c) the toilet.

Think about how you are feeling and whether you feel the same or different to what you were feeling before you found your partner. With your partner, discuss how you felt while looking around and how you think your partner felt.

Each child works on worksheet 23. The children put their completed worksheets on a wall.

Plan for using worksheet 24

Sense of self-worth

Aim   **For children to have sense of self worth.**

The facilitator explains how each person is unique and different from the next person.

Using worksheet 24 (in part 1), each child is to draw her or himself. Then that child or the child's friend can colour in the hair, eyes and so on, with the appropriate colours.

Encourage the children to share one or two pieces of information about their families. This can be done in groups where turn-taking can be practised. Comments should be kept positive.

Hello

I am a helper and this is

You

You have emotions, a body and a mind. Your emotions affect your body and your mind.

Talking does not use medicines.

Sometimes you can feel really bad about yourself. Talking can help you feel better about yourself.

Feeling good   Feeling bad

You can feel **bad**

Teacher saw me copy the sums.

if you break a rule.

5 ways to feel good

1 Eat well.

2 Exercise lots.

3 Play hard.

4 Sleep right.

5 Be Happy.

For a healthy body and mind you need to drink water and eat good food.

You need fresh air, daylight and exercise to grow strong and healthy.

You need to play with friends to learn how to get on with others.

You need to get enough sleep.
That's when you grow and heal.

Feel good about yourself so that you can be happy.

With your helper you can safely learn to understand your feelings.

Balance your life

Spend time with others.

Rest.

Be alone sometimes.

Learn something new.

Play fair.

Worksheet 19

The date is: _____   My name is: _____

Today I worked on: _____

It took me [   ] minutes to finish it.

I felt [   ] doing it.

{draw or write the feeling}

I felt [   ] when I did it.

{happy or sad face}

I know how to follow rules: Yes ☐ or No ☐

I have a friend called [   ]

I feel [   ]

I think that [   ]

What I want to do is [   ]

Jerry goes shopping

Jerry took something that did not belong to him, so he returned it.

What do you think Jerry did that was wrong?

What does your friend think Jerry did that was wrong?

What should Jerry have done instead?

What would you like as a present?

Draw Jerry.

Monique and her kitten

Little Monique leaves her house to find her kitten.

How did Monique's mum feel when she knew that Monique had left the house?

What could have Monique have done when she could not find her kitten?

What will Monique's mum say when they are back in the house?

Draw your favourite animal.

Clever Thomas

Thomas did not want to go to school because he was bullied.

Why did Thomas keep it a secret that he was called 'Fatty'?

How do you think he felt when he shared his problem?

What should happen next in the story?

Draw Clever Thomas.

Feel secure in setting

Draw and colour in something that is outdoors:

Draw and colour in something that is indoors:

Draw an apple and
colour it in:

Draw a pear and
colour it in:

Write your name: _____

Write the date: _____

Gain sense of self-worth

My name is: _____

My friend's name is: _____

Draw your face and ask your friend to colour it in.

Part Two

Talking is for Us: Emotional literacy for 8–12 year olds

Introduction
Record keeping and assessment
Stories and activities
Plans for using the worksheets
Worksheets

Introduction

Within the eight to twelve year age range, expect children to build on what they have already assimilated as follows: wait for what they want relatively easily, for example, turn-take; have the capacity to plan short-term goals, for example, learn a poem by heart to recite in class. They can also be expected to plan longer-term goals, such as revising for an examination and begin to discern whether to do something immediately or not, for example, watch a programme on television now or later. They should be able to understand that one problem can have different solutions, depending on one's perspective. At this stage of development, children can also be expected to ask for help, know and think about their emotions, deal with the emotions of others, listen to a story and answer questions about it appropriately.

For the eight to twelve year age range, research shows that fear of school, the dark, death, failure, criticism and home issues are prevalent (Scherer and Nakumara, 1968; Ollendick et al, 1985). Engaging in games which manifest externally what is inwardly processed is important for this age group. Brooking-Payne (1996) says that chasing games are especially important because they are a metaphor for the natural expression and contraction processes (for instance breathing), that govern living, as well as being a way to help stop being emotionally stunted. She recommends games such as the octopus and shark: One child is the shark, who says, "Swim little fish." The other children all run in the same direction: 'swimming' to the opposite wall without the shark catching them. If caught, they sit cross-legged on the floor and become octopuses. Once an octopus, a child can tag a fish who has yet not reached the opposite wall and that fish becomes an octopus.

The psychologist Martin Seligman (2005) discovered that teaching ten year olds optimism, reduced their rate of depression while going through puberty by 50 per cent. Negative emotions could be more easily handled and they started to understand the concept of self-talk.

Record keeping and assessment

Before the stories, activities and worksheets addressing some of these issues with a view to enhancing emotional literacy, there is an assessment form followed by a record sheet which are specifically for eight to twelve year olds. Further, worksheet 1 is in the form of a self-recording assessment and similarly, worksheet 2 is for a child to document an achievement; thus enabling the youngster in building an internal locus of evaluation.

Assessment form (to be filled in by the facilitator)

Child's name: ....

Aspects and skills	1st date	2nd date	3rd date
Feels safe in setting			
Has sense of self-esteem			
Is developing confidence			
Orientates self quickly in surroundings			
Respectful attitude to others			
Assumes she or he belongs			
Experiences achievements			
Readily expresses own needs and wants			
Can listen without interrupting			
Seems naturally honest			
Is empathic			
Can turn-take willingly			
Easily joins in group activities			
Interacts with others contentedly and fairly			
Copes with change without undue stress			
Works alone for 30 minutes			

My record (to be filled in by the young person)

My full name is ....

I worked on this sheet on (date): ....

This is how long it took me to finish it (write the number of minutes): ....

While doing it, I felt (write your feeling in the space below):

```
┌─────────────────────────────────────────────────────────────────┐
│                                                                   │
│                                                                   │
│                                                                   │
│                                                                   │
│                                                                   │
│                                                                   │
│                                                                   │
│                                                                   │
│                                                                   │
└─────────────────────────────────────────────────────────────────┘
```

I am pleased/not pleased (delete appropriately and draw how you felt in the space below) I did it.

```
┌─────────────────────────────────────────────────────────────────┐
│                                                                   │
│                                                                   │
│                                                                   │
│                                                                   │
└─────────────────────────────────────────────────────────────────┘
```

I do/do not know how to follow rules (delete appropriately).

I have a friend whose name is ....

At this moment I feel ....

What I think is ....

I want to ....

Stories and activities

Story 1
Cecil and the little creature

Once upon a time there was an old man who had a huge wart on his nose. He was short and skinny, with very wrinkled and baggy skin. He only had one tooth left in his mouth and that was dark brown. The old man looked extremely ugly. His name was Cecil.

One day Cecil felt hungry so he thought that he would quickly go to the shop at the corner of his road to buy some food. In his rush to go shopping, he forgot to lock the door to his bed-sitting room (where he lived). In his bed-sitting room, there was a large cage and inside the cage there was a beautiful tiny animal. Some people said, 'That's the most beautiful small animal I've ever seen'.

Cecil found the little animal in the middle of the road, with its tail torn off. He felt sorry for it, knowing that the creature would die if he left it there, so he took it to his bed-sitting room and kindly looked after it. Cecil soon realised that the creature had to be kept in a cage at all times, because it was so vicious. Even though Cecil was good to the animal, it still tried to bite him many times and scratch him viciously with its sharp claws.

While Cecil was out shopping, a ten year old girl was playing with her ball in the house where Cecil rented a bed-sitting room. The girl's name was Anna. Anna's ball accidentally hit Cecil's door. This made Cecil's door open and Anna thought, 'I wonder what's in there?' So she opened the door wide and did something naughty: she went inside.

Anna saw the beautiful little creature and opened the cage door. As soon as that happened, the animal attacked her. The girl had to go to hospital to recover from the attack. When Anna was better and out of hospital, she never went into a stranger's room again. Some people said, 'She's learnt her lesson the hard way'.

When Cecil returned to his bed-sitting room after going shopping, he felt very sorry that he left his door open, because of what happened to Anna. From that day onwards, Cecil remembered to lock his door whenever he went out.
(The originator of this story is Sophie Rudd, aged 11 years.)

Follow-up questions and activities for 'Cecil and the little creature'

Aims   To become aware of one's own emotion and to sense what another person is feeling, using art, intra-personal processing and interaction.

What did Anna do that was wrong?

What should Cecil have done before going shopping?

Was the little creature good or bad? Why?

Was the old man good or bad? Why?

Explain the saying, 'You can't judge a book by its cover'.

Find a partner. You think of one good thing and your partner thinks of one bad thing.

Make up a story with your partner incorporating one good and one bad thing.

Illustrate the story that you and your partner have made up (so you each write the same story) then your partner colours it in (so you each do your own illustration for your partner to colour in).

How did you feel when you were illustrating the story?

What do you think your partner felt when illustrating the story?

Worksheet 3 can be used with story 1.

Story 2
Yoko and the bully

Once upon a time there was a girl who was nearly eight years old. Her name was Yoko. English was her second language. She lived in a village in southern England and went to her local village primary school. Yoko was caring towards other individuals. Being a kind girl, she liked to help her teacher.

Abu was a boy in her class. He bullied her by calling her names, such as, 'Goody-gum-drops'. Occasionally, he poked her with his elbow. Although Abu was a noisy child, it was not easy for him to make good friends. His nick name was, 'The School Bully'.

One day, while Abu was playing by himself in the school playground, he tripped up and hurt his knee. The fall tore the skin on his knee and it was bleeding. It hurt so much that he cried big wet tears that rolled down his round cheek. Other children were also in the playground but they passed him by without any help, because they knew that he was a bully. Then Yoko saw him.

Yoko immediately went to help Abu. She went over to him and asked someone else to bring a teacher. Together, the teacher and Yoko helped Abu recover. They gently washed his knee in cold water to clean it and reduce the swelling, then put a plaster on his cut. Yoko and Abu spontaneously started to talk to each other. Yoko said, 'Don't worry, you'll be alright'.

They became very good friends and Abu stopped bullying Yoko. He liked having a friend that he could talk to and realised that if he stopped bullying and was caring, he could have good friends.

Follow up questions and activities for 'Yoko and the bully'

Aims to encourage creativity, promote listening skills, put one's self in the other person's shoes and increase emotional awareness, while intra-personally processing, using art, drama and interaction.

Think of the different ways that 'Yoko and the bully' could end then make up a different ending to the story.

How do you think Abu felt when he was hurt and no one came to help him?

Find a partner and tell you partner about a time when you helped another person.

Listen to your partner as she or he tells you about a time when she or he helped another person.

Make a drawing of the person who looks after you most of the time.
Let your partner colour in your drawing.
Act out the story of 'Yoko and the bully' with your partner.

Worksheet 4 can be used with story 2.

Story 3
The twin

For weeks, Mathew, who was nearly 12 years old, went to his drama club. He wanted to be in the yearly play, and be with his friends who were at the club and enjoyed his company. One day, his parents said, 'Mathew, we're going to Canada for the whole of your school summer holiday. You know we adopted you when you were three years old? Well, someone called Mark who lives in Canada has contacted us. Mark says that he was adopted when he was 12 weeks old and that he is your biological twin brother. He has tracked down where you live and he wants to meet us all. He wants to meet the whole family.'

Mathew felt angry that his parents decided to take him with them for a long summer holiday, to meet a stranger who said that he was his twin. Mathew shouted, 'Oh no! The drama club's doing a play in the summer holiday and I want to be in it. If I go to Canada it means that I can't be in it. I won't see my friends either. How can you do this to me?'

His parents tried to calm him down, saying, 'This seems like a chance of a life time. You'll meet someone your own age, who's longing to meet with you and be a special friend to you. Mathew, it's your twin. You can see your old friends every day at school. Don't worry about the drama club. You'll get a chance to be in a play next year.'

Mathew's heart was thumping so hard he thought that it would jump out of his chest. He wanted to scream, 'Just do what I want!' He did not scream. Instead of that, he kept quiet and clenched his jaw while frowning. Pouting heavily, he shut himself in his bedroom, feeling that life was unfair towards him.

(I am grateful to Maria, my eldest daughter, for giving me the idea for this story.)

Follow-up activities for 'The twin'

Aims To link thought with feeling, be empathic, listen actively and use imagination, interaction, drama and process interpersonally.

How do you think Mathew felt about meeting his estranged twin?
Find a partner and tell your partner about a time when you did something brave.
Describe how you felt.
Listen to your partner as she or he tells you about a time when they did something brave.

After listening to how she or he felt, repeat back to your partner what you have just been told.

With your partner, decide on a different ending to Mathew's story.

Role-play a happy ending to 'The twin', with your partner.

Worksheet 5 can be used with story 3.

Story 4
Pollyanna's ninth birthday

Once upon a time there was a girl called Pollyanna. It was her ninth birthday party. Pollyanna's grandfather looked after her. He said that she could have three friends for an afternoon tea party.

The birthday tea consisted of peanut butter sandwiches, pieces of apple, cake and fizzy drinks. Her grandfather put on some music and each of the friends gave Pollyanna a present. She said, 'Thank you', to each friend, as she took the presents. The friends watched her open them with wide-eyed pleasure.

All the friends were in her class. They were: Yanni, he sat next to her; Sam, she sat at the next table to hers in the classroom and Josephine. Josephine played with Pollyanna every break time at school. All the friends played well together and whenever there was an argument, they always made up afterwards. Each friend was happy when they were good together.

After the tea party Pollyanna's friends went to their homes and her grandfather gave her a present. It was a purse. She had wanted a purse for a long time and was very happy with it. In fact, it became her favourite object. Each time she looked at it, she experienced a feeling of contentment. She looked at it every day.

Pollyanna was usually very good at getting up in time to go to school in the mornings. Indeed, she was so good at it that she would wake up before her grandfather. One morning, she did not wake up before the grandfather because she had stayed up later than usual to watch the end of a film on the television, the night before. On that morning, her grandfather went into her room to wake her up and noticed that she liked the purse so much, that she slept with it on her bed. This touched her grandfather so much that he put a special note in her lunch box on that day. Pollyanna found it during her lunch-break and read it out loud: 'I'm proud of you'. She was pleased that her grandfather was proud of her.

Follow-up stories and activities for 'Pollyanna's ninth birthday'

Aims To be aware of one's own emotion, to communicate with others, show appreciation and use cognitive processes to problem solve while interacting, using art, drama and intra-personally processing.

What is your favourite object?
With at least one other person discuss how you would feel, what you would think and do, if you could not find your favourite object.
Imagine that Pollyanna's home had been left dirty and untidy after the party. What do you think she and her grandfather would do?

On your own, think of all the ways that you can clean and tidy up.

If Pollyanna has to cross a road by herself to get to school, what is the safest way for her to cross it?

Find a partner. Does your partner agree with the answer you gave to the above question?

Each pair join with another (so that there are about four people to a group) and act out the story of 'Pollyanna's ninth birthday'. Groups can show one another their playlet and appreciation can be shown with applause.

On a sheet of paper, your partner can draw the grandfather on half of it; you draw Pollyanna on the other half. Co-operate to do this, work together not one at a time.

Worksheet 6 can be used with story 4.

Story 5
The school hamster

Fluffy was the name of a hamster that was kept at a primary school. A boy called Aaron was the hamster monitor. That meant that he had to look after the hamster every day at school, before the lessons started.

One day, Aaron was ill and did not go to school. On that day, his teacher had to do extra work at school, because she took care of Fluffy. She did not like doing the extra work and complained to the head-teacher. The head-teacher said, 'Leave the problem with me; I'll see to it.'

That day, she wrote a letter to every parent whose child went to the school. The letter informed the parents that the school was unable to look after Fluffy and unless the hamster had a new home, it would be sent to a vet who would kill it. It seemed that no one wanted Fluffy except Aaron. Aaron begged his mum and dad for the hamster and promised to clean its cage, give it food, water and play with it daily.

His parents said firmly, 'It's not fair on the hamster. If we get the animal, then we won't be able to go for the weekends away that we're used to because there'd be no one here to take care of Fluffy. That's why we can't have the hamster.'

Aaron thought very hard about this. He did not miserably give up his vision of having a hamster. Instead, he thought of his situation as a problem to solve. He thought that perhaps he could quickly destroy the hamster but soon changed his mind, knowing that that would not only be cruel, but also extremely upsetting. Then he thought that he might steal the hamster and hide it. However, he told himself that this would be a very naughty thing to do and that if he did do that, people would not trust him any more. After all these negative thoughts, he started thinking of positive possibilities. His best idea was to get a friend who lived nearby and loved looking after animals, to take care of Fluffy, whenever he and his parents went away for more than 24 hours. Full of hope, Aaron told his parents his best positive idea. His mum and dad stood in silence for what seemed like a long time. At last, they said that Aaron could have Fluffy. He was delighted! The school gave Aaron the hamster. He looked after it every day and when he was not able to, his friend looked after Fluffy. Fluffy lived to a contented and healthy old age.

Follow-up questions and activities for 'The school hamster'

Aims   Linking thought and feeling, art, intra-personal processing and interaction.

Find a partner. Tell the story of 'The school hamster', using your own words. Where do you think you can find information on how to look after a hamster?

Make a list of all the things that you do to look after yourself.
If your mother was sick in bed and you had to take care of her, what would you think and do?
How would you feel?
Make a comic strip of the story 'The school hamster'.
Let your partner colour in your comic strip.

Worksheet 7 can be used with story 5.

Plans for the worksheets

If there is no separate plan for using a worksheet, then the worksheet itself is self-explanatory.

Plan for using worksheet 3

Favourite pet

Aim   Environmental awareness and learning to learn.

Ensure that the children each have a copy of worksheet 3.
Each child thinks about what it would be like if no one took care of them.
Ask each child to think about the last time they had something to eat or drink.
Ask each child, 'What is your favourite pet?' Listen to the answer and acknowledge it.
The children all move around as if they are their favourite animal and make animal music: i.e. make the sound of the animal that they like best. At a given cue, they freeze as if they have to have a photograph taken. You may take a photograph of them if you have immediate access to printing copies of it, and use the photograph as a springboard for discussion with the children. They could also each take a copy of the photograph home to show their parents/ guardians and talk about what they did with you, if they wish.
The children fill in worksheet 3.
The children form small groups and talk about the individuals who look after them.
In small groups, make up a little play about going shopping and finding a surprise when you get home.
Watch each group perform (up to two minutes per group) and show your appreciation with applause.

Plan for using worksheet 4

Let's talk

Aim   For children to understand how to change a negative emotion into a positive one, know their emotions, manage them, express their feelings, cope with a relationship, be social and experience positive affect.

Ensure that all the children each have a copy of worksheet 4.

Ask the children what happens when they feel angry.

Ask the children how they feel when they are laughing.

Each child works on worksheet 4.

Ask the children to find a partner and show by the movement of their bodies, that they are angry with their partner, then ask them to change their movements to show that they have calmed down.

Tell the children to make a sound (not a word, for example, they could make a humming sound), with their partners, which depicts calmness.

Each pair may have a different sound so ask each pair to make their sound in turn; in this way all the children can listen to everyone's sound. In this way, the children make their own calmness-sounds and or music which can be recorded and played back to them.

Plan for using worksheet 5

Recognise feelings

Aim   For children to have a sense of self-worth and be happy while working independently and being sensitive to their own as well as someone else's feelings.

Ensure that all children have a copy of worksheet 5.

Ask the children to close their eyes and imagine receiving a present. At this point, each child can experience her or his own emotion.

The children find a partner and discuss how they felt when receiving a present, before continuing.

With eyes shut, the children imagine giving a present to someone and seeing that person's response.

Using only movement with no words, each child finds a partner and all the pairs mime giving one another a present.

The children discuss in pairs, what they think that a person feels when receiving a present.

Fill in worksheet 5.

Plan for using worksheet 6

The present

Aim   Thinking of others, being self-aware, learning to learn and environmental awareness.

Ensure that the children each have a copy of worksheet 6.

Read through worksheet 6.

With partners, the children discuss what they would like to put into worksheet 6.

The children take ten seconds with their eyes closed to get in touch with how they are feeling at this moment, before getting into small groups to make up a song about how they are feeling in relation to worksheet 6. Each group can perform to the others who listen before showing appreciation by moving their bodies and arms (altogether) on the spot, in a way which reflects how the song makes them feel; so each child may have a different movement.

Fill in worksheet 6

Plan for using worksheet 7

Liking and smiling

Aim **Practising positive feedback, being able to listen and gain a sense of self-worth.**

Think about what some one might need in order to be healthy.
Think about what makes you happy.
Fill in worksheet 7.

Plans for using worksheets A to R
'Belinda gets help'

About these worksheets
These illustrated worksheets unfold the story of a school child between the ages of eight and twelve, who has an emotional problem which is dealt with in a proper manner. It also describes a dream that a young cat has where there is a difficulty which is resolved via mediation. It is a simple yet imaginative story with some sadness which ends happily. The purpose of the main story is to show that an undesirable situation can be resolved. Although the cat's dream may appear as separate from the story, it is actually linked. This is because there is a parallel process between what happens in the dream and the main story.

Reasons for the alphabetically ordered sheets
The alphabetically marked pages are ordered in such a way that they tell a story in their own right, irrespective of the previous numbered ones.

Introduction to the story
All children will have experienced both positive and negative emotions, as does the girl in the story. We do not know the reason for the girl's sad state, but we

do know that by interacting with a special helper, which includes talking, she gets better. This is the process that the young cat's dream reflects. By reading the narrative, acting it out and talking about it, it may be possible for children not only to relate the situation to a similar experience in their lives, where talking helped them to solve a problem, but also to identify with the emotions of others, such as the characters in the story. Children can work independently by reading the story individually, to themselves. By letting them read to the end of the story, you will be facilitating them to feel the positive emotion that the outcome of the story ends on. It is not unusual to discover a solution to a problem during a discussion. That is one reason why being able to express oneself is important. This is a reason why talking is encouraged. Sometimes, changes within the home and school environment can cause behavioural problems. We can only imagine what changes occurred which the girl in the story reacted to by staying in bed and crying. However, relevant support that included talking, enabled her to move in a desired direction.

Aim For children to express themselves in a structured and creative way, to experience positive emotion, work independently and identify with the emotions of others.

Prepare sheets A to R into a booklet so that each child has a copy.

Children take turns to read aloud the story on the sheets.

First one child reads page A, then the next child reads page B, after that another child reads page C and so on, until the whole narrative has been read by the class or group of children who are involved in this activity.

In pairs, each child tells the story to their partner, using their own words to describe what has been read out. (This facilitates a way for children to express themselves creatively yet in a structured way.) The partner listens. Children who listened, repeat back, using their own words if they wish, what they heard their partners saying. (This facilitates respectful listening towards the first person who created their own words to tell the story which has been read out.) Such a process can take up a whole lesson or part of a lesson. You decide what is best for your children.

The story is acted out, see below. (For this, the class room can be arranged in such a way that there is a 'performance' area and an 'audience' area.)

In groups, the groups simultaneously take about seven minutes to decide how they will act out the story. However, instead of speaking, they can sing the words, and instead of moving as they do in daily life, they can move more fluidly, as if they are dancing.

Each group's performance can last for approximately three minutes. At a given moment in time (the facilitator decides on the exact moment) the children close their eyes for a few moments to become more fully aware of how they feel in-the-moment; then they continue creating a performance when the facilitator gives them a signal to carry on.

The class may watch each group performing, then applaud. (In my experience, this is tremendous fun and the children love doing it.)

Each child can make her or his own book about emotions, which includes illustrations. This step can be follow-on work, perhaps for homework.

Further follow-on work: Colour in the sheets, perhaps take the sheets home to colour in. Children can start this activity in the class (or session room) if there is time, and any colouring medium can be used (e.g. paint).

Aims **to introduce, recognise and talk about emotions, as experienced by the characters that are in the illustrated story within sheets A to R. (The ideas need not take up a whole session or lesson. Depending on the ability of the children, the ideas can be used within a term's work and each lesson or session, or part of a lesson or session, can focus on one or two [depending on time] of the sheets marked from A to R.)**

Idea 1   After reading the story choose any sheet to print or copy for each child. The children discuss in groups what might have happened before and after what is on the sheets, which is different to the actual story. The groups may each have a different perspective, so a co-operative, fun and friendly way to share the ideas is to role play their ideas to the rest of the other groups. In this way, it may take a substantial part of an academic term to work through these sheets.

Idea 2   Activities during the role play can keep the children's interest if they are given the opportunity to role play not only the human characters and animals in the story, but also inanimate objects such as the girl's bedroom door. Then, the child who enacts an inanimate object can be asked imaginative questions such as, 'As the door of the girl's room, how did you feel when you realised that you were not used very much because the girl just stayed in her bed?' or/and, 'How would you have liked the girl to have used you, as the door?' or/and, 'What do you think the cat could do in the story?' and so on. In this way, the children can think about their acting, about problems and find solutions. They will also be using their imagination while not criticising others, but will be building on the views of others.

Idea 3   In their groups, the children can discuss topics such as, 'What makes me sad?' and 'What can bring happiness?' These and other discussion topics they and you may like to include can help the children develop their listening skills, understand and recognise emotions and see how they are linked to behaviour.

Plan for using worksheet S

Aim   Sense of self-worth, feel secure, keep sight of own needs and gain confidence.

Ensure that each child has a copy of worksheet S.

The facilitator informs the children that although all humans have similarities, each person is also unique and without such uniqueness the world would be a very boring place to live in.

The children discuss, in positive terms, how they are the same and different from one another.

Each child fills in sheet S before it is stapled together to make a booklet incorporating sheets A to S.

Record of assessment

Fill in what you think you are good at and what you could improve on in the blank spaces.

Name…..................................... Date…...............................

Any other comment…............…...............

Skills

I'm good at …........................… when …...........................

I can improve on…........................ if …...............................

I'm good at …........................… when …...........................

I can improve on…........................ if …...............................

I'm good at …........................… when …...........................

I can improve on…........................ if …...............................

I'm good at …........................... when …...........................

I can improve on…........................ if …...............................

I'm good at …........................… when …...........................

Achievement

My name is: _____ and I like to be called: _____

What I have done that I am proud of is: _____

What I am pleased with is: _____ because: _____

Before doing it I felt: _____ While doing it I felt:_____

This is a drawing of how I felt after I did it :

I think that if I: _____ then: _____

What I want to do is: _____ because:_____

The date I finished working on this sheet is: _____

It took me: _____ to finish it.

Favourite pet

How would you feel if you left your room and when you returned you found an injured stranger in it?

I would feel_____

Cecil is an old man. How old is the most elderly person that you know?

The oldest person I know is approximately _____ years old.

What should Cecil do before shopping, to stop intruders entering his property?

Cecil should _____

What would you like as a favourite pet and how would you take care of it? _____
_____

Draw old Cecil:

This is Cecil.

Let's talk

Draw a situation that makes you feel good:

Find a partner, talk about your drawing with your partner.

Write down what you do to calm down when you are angry:

_____

_____

With a partner, explain to one another what makes you feel happy, then write down your explanation:

_____

_____

Recognise feelings

Joey gives Gemma a toy she has wanted for a long time. In the space provided, write down how she feels then draw the situation before colouring it in.

Draw happiness.

The present

Think of someone you love and make a drawing of that person:

If that person gave you a present what would your behavioural response be ? What would you do ?

_____

How would you feel?

_____

What would you say?

_____

What would be two inappropriate responses?

_____

_____

Liking and smiling

Tell someone what you like about them.

Ask someone to explain how she or he feels when smiling. Listen to the answer.

Either draw yourself smiling or a shape that represents joy to you:

Belinda gets help.

Hello! My name is Kitty.
My owner Belinda is
very unhappy.

Belinda's Mummy makes an appointment for her to see someone to help her.

She gets help by visiting a special helper.

On the way to the helper, I bump into Olu and Pepi.

During Belinda's session she shares the helper's things such as art equipment and soft toys.

While Belinda is with Yoko,
Kitty goes to sleep and
happily dreams.

Kitty dreams she is playing with Pepi in the long grass.

Kitty feels pleased with the session.

So do Olu and Pepi.

"Wake up Kitty!"

My name is ...

I am ... years old.

My friend's name is ...

My teacher's name is ...

My favourite drink is ...

My favourite food is ...

My favourite game is ...

I like ...

When I grow up
I want to be a ...

Part Three

Talking is for Teens: Emotional literacy for 13–19 year olds

Introduction
Record keeping and assessment
Stories and activities
Plans for using the worksheets
Worksheets

Introduction

Within 13 to 19 year age range, expect teenagers to build on what they have previously assimilated, talk about how they feel without blaming others, be aware of emotions in others during conversation, manage conflict in relationships, know the difference between emotion, thought and behaviour, plan goals from short to long-term, for example: From planning what to do this evening, to planning how to launch themselves into the career of their choice. Also expect teenagers to review their progress, for example, by assessing choices made in the past to see if they are working out as planned and if not, to make necessary changes. Further, expect teenagers to delay gratification to achieve their goals, such as, not spend money on music, magazines, clothes or on going out but save it to have enough for a holiday. Expect them to continue to learn ways of dealing with emotions, such as being assertive, using self talk, relaxation and visualization. Also expect empathy, the ability to see each person's point of view, and make up their own minds if, when and how they respond to another. They also should keep healthy boundaries between themselves and others; and identify the more subtle emotions, such as embarrassment and jealousy in self and others.

If teenagers feel that they are the stars of their lives, they are healthily self-empowered (Harrill, 1996). According to Harrill, they need to experience being in charge of what they do, what they say and what they feel. She explains that in this way, they can change parts of their life paths that they do not like, to something more positive for themselves. Adolescents, as well as older teenagers (16–19 year olds) can therefore empower themselves. One way for teens to be self-empowered is for them to be aware of their own needs, to know where to get their needs met and to create a precise action plan of how to get those needs met (Harrill, 1966). For example:

- I want to be physically healthier
- A nutritionist would help me learn about eating healthily
- I could also take an exercise class three times a week and be in bed by 10. pm. on most nights.

By taking charge of their own lives they can empower themselves, build their self-esteem and increase emotional literacy. Many teenagers are riddled with self-doubt. During the years between 13 and 19 inclusively, many emotional problems are rooted in unresolved traumas during middle childhood resulting from being susceptible to impressionability and openness. Teenagers 'should be encouraged to work through potential crises. This is a vital age, where many of the old structures ... begin to be discarded. Adult instructions and guidance ...

questioned. What is of great importance is that activities that build a new emotional structure and security are engaged in' (Brooking-Payne, p. 57).

Brooking-Payne declares that a teenager's process needs to be recognized by a formalized outward structure which relates to an 'initiation' or 'rite of passage'. She states that games, such as, sports, can do this. Psychologists Olsen and Sutton's (1998) investigation into teenagers focused on those aged 14 to 19. Results from their work showed that the less positive the teenagers found relationships, the more they tended to become isolated with the implication that support would not be sought at a time when they needed help for a physical illness; in the case of this research, diabetes. Good emotional literacy allows teenagers to deal with such issues.

Record keeping and assessment

If you decide to have a programme to use the worksheets in, assessment is recommended as well as record keeping. To keep records, store all the evidence you collect. This can be done by photocopying and filing the worksheets which the teenagers have worked on. For assessing purposes, there is a suggested assessment form below.

Assessment form

Participant's name ....

Works alone for 45 minutes ....

Accommodates change ....

Interacts appropriately ....

Can delay gratification ....

Empathic ....

Accepting of others ....

Honest ....

Voluntarily expresses needs and wants ....

Experiences achieving ....

Self-esteem ....

Feels secure ....

Stories and activities

The following fifteen stories and activities facilitate teenagers to investigate different facets of developing emotionally. Story form can be used safely with teens to explore emotional issues. The format for the stories and activities section is

- A story
- Activities
- Worksheets.

Worksheets are designed for independent use; they do not need to be used with a story.

Stories 1–15 can either be read to the youngsters or copied for them to read. You will notice that many of the activities involve the participants collaborating. This is a crucial part of this project so it is advised that co-operative activities are encompassed in every session. All the stories involve an aspect that many teenagers face.

Story number	Related issue
1	smoking
2	drug abuse
3	pregnancy
4	dropping out
5	violence
6	disease
7	impulse control
8	managing anger
9	solution to a predicament
10	sadness
11	jealousy
12	pride
13	guilt
14	anxiety
15	alcohol

The cartoon style is a deliberate attempt to provide neutral pictures that contain little specific information thus ensuring the participants bring their own experiences without being influenced by detailed illustrations.

Story 1
Smoking

John's parents were lifelong smokers. When John was born, he turned out to be genetically modified to deal with continual intake of vile, toxic smoke: no hair to get in the way of a cigarette, small eyes so that they would not become easily irritated by smoke, extra large nose and lungs to cope with continuous irritation. Is this a marvel of modern breeding? 'Pass the fags!' he seemed to automatically say. No-one responded. He had to get his own fags. He dropped the fag ends on the floor. People felt nauseated by his noxious smoker's breath. Nobody went near him. Everyone wanted him to co-operate with their feelings and only smoke in private. This would at least show that he was behaving with some responsibility.

(This story is by Dr. S. A. Rudd)

Follow-up questions and activities for 'Smoking'

Aims   Identify, name and express emotions, problem-solve, become aware of environment and deal with a health issue using art, intra-personal processing and interaction.

Use your imagination and creativity to help make a drawing of John.
What are the hazards of throwing cigarette ends on the floor?
How do you think John felt when he realized that no-one wanted to be close to him?
In groups of three to six people, brainstorm ways that John can stop smoking.
One person in each group writes down everything that is brainstormed.
Members of your group collaboratively decide on a plan, which is gleaned from the brainstorming ideas, for John to stop smoking.
The plan is written on a sheet of paper and each of the groups explains their plan to the other groups.
What were your feelings while reading the story?
Make a painting of the emotions you felt.

Worksheets 1 and 2 can be used with story 1.

Story 2
Drug abuse

Sue had the reputation of being a rebel. From a young age, she hid her feelings. As she grew into her middle childhood years, feelings of sadness or anger were ignored by her and she did nothing to stop feeling such emotions. By the time she was a teenager she started experimenting with drugs. She went from tobacco to alcohol to illegal soft drugs and then to hard ones.

'I'm not an addict. You think I've got a problem with controlling myself but I can stop any time I want; I just don't want to 'cos I don't feel like it'. That is what 19 year old Sue said to her counsellor. Sue's counsellor sighed as he left the counselling rehabilitation unit, after hearing the latest news about Sue. 'I just don't want to' had echoed inside his head, since he heard that she was dead. Not an addict, she could stop any time she wanted to? The counsellor felt very sad indeed.

(This story is by Dr. S. A. Rudd)

Follow-up questions and activities for story 'Drug abuse'

Aims   Delay gratification, control impulse, problem-solve, learn how to learn, see a different perspective and reduce stress, using intra-personal processing, interaction and music.

How do you think Sue's parents reacted to the news of her death? Think about this but do not share your thoughts until you have worked through the next five points.

Remember a minor loss that you have had (for example losing a key).

Recollect how stressed you felt about your loss.

Think about what helped you with the feeling of loss or what would have helped you in reducing the stress you experienced.

Play a piece of music which sounds stressy.

After the above bulleted point, change the music to a piece which induces relaxation.

In groups of three to six people, brainstorm ways that Sue could have stopped herself from becoming a drug addict, if you feel as if you want to exclude an idea someone puts forward, control this by stopping yourself because all ideas are accepted during brainstorming.

118

One person in each group writes down everything that is brainstormed.

Members of each group collaboratively decide on a plan, which is gleaned from the brainstorming ideas, on how Sue could have saved herself from death due to her abuse of drugs. Write the plan on a piece of paper.

Each group then explains its plan to the other groups.

Worksheets 3 and 4 can be used with story 2.

Story 3
Pregnancy

Josh, aged six months, wailed inconsolably in the night. This was not unusual for him. His father was 17 year old Trevor, who worked on his late shift at McAdams-Burgers. He usually worked late so that he could take home a little more money than if he worked the more sociable hours. At work, Trevor was the four star employee of the month, so he could command a little more than the legal minimum wage per hour. This was less than the child minder charged him when his step-mother would not look after Josh.

Walking home after his shift he finished eating his free McAdams-Burger before impulsively throwing his rubbish on the ground. Trevor wondered how things might have been if Sharon and he had been more careful and used self-control, or used contraception, or even if she had not died after the caesarian operation. 'Blood clot', they said. Trevor thought, 'Perhaps we should have waited until we were older. Oh Sharon, I felt so sexy when you flirted with me. Was it worth it? You wanted the baby as well, didn't you?'

Now at home, Josh is still wailing. He seems to have a fever. Trevor's step-mother is 'out to the world', drunk. Trevor thinks he should call the GP to get Josh checked. His next McAdams shift is at 10.00 am As usual, Trevor will not sleep much before going to work again. Although he wants to watch the very late night film on television, he uses some self-control and goes to bed instead. This is how problematic Trevor's life is now; he does not know where to ask for help, or how to solve what he thinks of as his 'big problem of life'.

(This story is by Dr S. A. Rudd)

Follow-up questions and activities for 'Pregnancy'

Aims   Look at the issue of pregnancy, enhance environmental awareness, know that behaviour is not the same as emotion, be able to verbalise, understand non-verbal communication and problem solve using intra-personal processing, interaction and movement.

What do you think Trevor's thoughts are on teenage sex?
How do you think Trevor feels regarding teenage sex?
In what way do you think that Trevor behaves with reference to what he thinks and feels about teenage sex?
In pairs, discuss ways in which you think Trevor can improve his life.
In groups, act out the above story with a different ending which you make up with your group; do not use any words – show what you want to communicate by using mime.

Groups show one another their enactments of the above.
Acknowledge each group's performance by moving in a way which shows your appreciation.

Worksheets 5 and 6 can be used with story 3.

Story 4
Dropping out

I had a friend called Julian. Julian did not like school, so he left earlier than most, but he could not find any work. I felt sorry for him so I helped him get his first job. It was as a farm labourer. He quickly learnt practical farm skills: mucking out the pigs, ploughing, digging, putting fences up and so on. I saw him once, ten years later, digging a hole for farmer Giles. After that, I did not see him at all for a long time, maybe until we were both about 50 years old.

Julian still worked the land but had moved on from farmer Giles to farmer Brown, yet he was doing the same routine: digging, fencing, mucking out, etc. I spoke with him for a while, then left. It seems odd, when we were boys at school he was just as bright as me. I wondered if he could have made a bit more of himself, when he said to me that he felt bored being in a 'dead end' job. Julian also disclosed that he often wondered how things would have turned out if he had not dropped out but stayed on at school with me all those years ago.

(This story is by Dr. S. A. Rudd)

Follow up questions and activities for 'Dropping out'

Aims   Self-talk, social development, environmental awareness and problem-solving using intra-personal processing, interaction and drama.

How do you think Julian behaved towards his friend when they met in their fifties?

Tell yourself what you think Julian would be saying to himself after meeting his friend in his fifties.

In pairs, discuss how Julian's life might have been different if he had continued with his education all those years ago.

If Julian does not want to be in a dead-end job, how do you think he could get out of it?

What advice would you give a 16 year old who does not want to learn anything, but stays in bed all day, eats junk food take-aways and throws the rubbish on the floor?

In small groups, act out a good-for-nothing youngster who realizes where she or he may be heading by a chance meeting with a wise person and show the young person's 'journey' from a meaningless to a meaningful life.

Each group shows its performance to the other groups who make their appreciation clear by applauding the performances.

Worksheet 7 can be used with story 4.

Story 5
Violence

When Sebastian was 17 years old his college organized a disco for his year group. There were over 100 17-year-olds all seemingly having a good time at the disco. Sebastian had danced many dances. His heart was thumping quickly, he was out of breath, sweaty, very hot and tired. He wanted to sit down and have a drink.

Sebastian went to buy himself an orange juice but they were sold out. He went to find a chair to sit on but they were all taken. He decided to go and sit on the toilet but that was engaged. Feeling angry about his experiences, he suddenly thrust his fist into a closed window. The glass shattered and cut his hand. Although his hand healed, his lecturers remained concerned about his violent episode, so in his report they wrote, 'Sebastian seems to have a problem with violence'. Two years later, Sebastian was not accepted at any institution to work, because when prospective employers saw 'Sebastian seems to have a problem with violence', they did not want to have anything to do with him.

Eventually, he befriended a group of violent people and ended up in prison for physically attacking someone whom he felt annoyed by.

Follow up questions and activities for 'violence'

Aims Understand others, know the difference between proper and improper behaviour, be positive, appropriately emotionally expressive and self-aware using intra-personal processing and interaction.

> What is it like when you feel happy?
> If you see a man crying, what might he be feeling?
> Violence hurts and so can some words. What words might be hurtful?
> Why is it a bad idea to be violent?
> In groups of three to six people, think of non-violent ways in which Sebastian could have dealt with his anger.
> Appoint a scribe in your group who writes down all the ideas.
> What were your thoughts, feelings and actions while you appointed a scribe?
> Put the paper where all the groups can see it.
> Everybody should then read all of the ideas to themselves, and think of at least one good and honest thing to say about them.
> Discussion can follow on.

Worksheet 8 can be used with the story 5.

Story 6
Disease

'Didn't you learn about sexually transmitted diseases?' (STDs.) That question screamed silently inside teenaged Mazemine's head while she lovingly and gently touched her 40 year old mother's arm, now limp, as she lay between clean, white, hospital sheets. Normally, Hazel was a lively and noisy mother.

Each morning she happily sang with a full-throated voice. Mazemine remembered how she exclaimed, 'Oh mum, shut-up!' Now, oh how she missed her mother's out of tune singing. She even missed her mother's embarrassing liveliness. Mazemine wished she had told her mother many times that she loved her. She wished many things. Most of all, she wished she had told her about STDs.

Mazemine learnt about STDs at school, how easily they were transmitted and that in particular (as in her mother's case), chlamydia, which is caused by bacteria transmitted during sex. In women, this often has no symptoms, or very mild ones such as cramping or tenderness in the pelvic floor or abdomen, and perhaps bleeding between periods, nausea and fever. Men also may not have symptoms. Although antibiotics can cure chlamydia if treated early, if left untreated it can grow into a more serious illness: pelvic inflammatory disease (PID). Her mother had not been taught these facts. Consequently, she was now lying in a hospital bed. The infection had spread to her fallopian tubes and she had considerable pain. Indeed, Hazel's fallopian tubes were now scarred, so she could never get pregnant again. Hazel's case was severe, requiring a hospital stay.

Sitting at her mother's bedside, Mazemine remembered her mother asking, 'What did you learn at school today?' How she regretted not telling her mother what she had learnt about STDs. Especially chlamydia! Mazemine was left wondering about her mother's sexual partner. Did she have more than one? He or they must be told and be treated or they could pass STD back to Hazel or possibly someone else!

Follow up questions and activities for 'Disease'

Aims Problem-solve, boost confidence, identify where to ask for help, understand a different person's point of view using intra-personal processing and interaction.

How do you think an STD is transmitted?
Think about who you can talk to if you have a problem.
In pairs, discuss the type of person whom you feel you can share a problem with.

In pairs, tell each other about a problem you have had and how you coped with it.

With your partner, think of two problems that a teenager might face, then brainstorm who that teenager can get help from for each of the problems.

Worksheets 9 and 10 can be used with story 6.

Story 7
Impulse control

A group of young individuals were challenged. The challenge was called 'The Marshmallow Test'. This is what it involved:

Their teacher said, 'I have to go out for 15–20 minutes. I am putting some marshmallows on the table. You can have one each now but, whoever does not have one now and can wait until I return can have two marshmallows as soon as I come back'. Some of the young individuals immediately snatched the marshmallow and ate it. The others however, waited for what seemed like an endless, 15-20 minutes. They found waiting for their teacher such a difficult task that they thought of ways to avoid temptation. These ways included covering their eyes, putting their heads in their arms, singing songs and playing games. Eventually the teacher returned and they were rewarded with two marshmallows.

These preschoolers were four years old. There was a later follow up on the youngsters when they were aged 14, 16 and as adults. The outcome of the research was that the participants who displayed impulse control at age four, were as teenagers, more adept, had more positive personal impact, more confidence and were better able to cope with life's stresses than the ones who could not control their impulses. Indeed, even at the age of 26 years, the participants that had displayed impulse control were competent, assertive, psychologically robust and able to pursue their goals for a reward worth waiting for, unlike many of the others.

(Goleman, 1995, references this experiment, undertaken by Walter Mischel.)

Follow up questions and activities for 'Impulse control'

Aims   Control impulses, support moral development and delay gratification using intra-personal processing, interaction and art.

What helps you control your impulses?
In groups of three to six, think of ways in which impulses can be controlled. Appoint a spokesperson in your group to tell the other groups the ways that your group thought of for controlling impulses.

Worksheet 11 can be used with story 7.

Story 8
Managing Anger

Ross was 60 years old and in hospital because he had suffered from a heart attack that morning while making a sandwich for his son Jojo who had come to visit him. Jojo was newly married and had not seen his father for a relatively long time. This is because Ross would get angry at Jojo throughout his growing years and even his adult life and hit him if he did not do as he was told.

Jojo's wife Nikki, however, felt sure that Ross loved his son but that he had a problem with managing his anger. Jojo agreed with his wife so he decided to visit his father. Ross was overjoyed by Jojo's visit and wanted to show Jojo that he loved him very much. The only way he could think of doing this was by offering him food which is why he was making the sandwiches. He also felt angry and wanted to shout at Jojo because Jojo had dropped his coat by the front door instead of hanging it on a peg. Ross' face looked contorted with anger. Underneath that angry exterior was a pure love for his son which was locked inside him and that he longed to release. Unfortunately, he did not know how. Then Ross had the heart attack.

How tragic that neither Ross nor Jojo had any information about the link between being inept at managing anger and having a heart attack.

Follow up questions and activities for 'Managing anger'

Aims Identify, name and assess level of emotion, develop socially and problem-solve using intra-personal processing, interaction and music.

How did you learn your way of dealing with anger?
In groups, brainstorm positive anger management techniques.
Find some music which sounds angry and play it. Describe as closely as you can, how it makes you feel.
Find some music which sounds soothing and play it. Describe as closely as you can how it makes you feel.

Worksheet 12 can be used with story 8.

Story 9
A solution to a predicament

Jade was 19 years old and there was a boy at her college called Mark whom she liked very much. He could be described as her boyfriend. They did not see each other outside college hours because much of their free time was spent studying for exams.

Jade's best friend was Louise. Louise's mother had re-married and given birth to a baby girl. Every Saturday evening, Louise babysat for her mother. 'Jade, please can you come over this Saturday and keep me company? I'm so fed up babysitting on my own on Saturdays.' That is what Louise said to Jade on the telephone. Jade answered her saying, 'Yes, of course I'll come over Louise. I'll bring a DVD that we can watch'. 'Thanks, Jade!' responded Louise.

Later that evening, Mark telephoned Jade saying, 'Hi Jade! Let's take a break from studying this Saturday evening. Can I come over to your place and bring a DVD we can watch?' Every pore on Jade's body wanted to yell out, 'Oh yes please, come over on Saturday evening Mark!' She kept quiet, however, not wanting to let Louise down or break her word to her.

Jade was in a social predicament and needed to find a positive solution to her problem. She thought, 'What am I to do? I want to be in two places at the same time with two different people who have both asked for my company.' She thought over her problem. Jade thought of various solutions such as: pretending to forget the meeting with Louise, or tell Louise a lie to get out of seeing her. Jade did not feel comfortable with these two solutions because they were negative, so she started to think positively. Jade thought of another two possible options. Firstly, she could tell Mark that she had a previous engagement and arrange to see him another time. Secondly, that he could join her at Louise's, on the condition that Louise felt fine about this. Her final decision came easily.

She eventually decided to honour her word to help Louise with babysitting and to tell her boyfriend that if Louise was fine about it they could all watch his DVD at Louise's place. Louise was happy with this arrangement. In this way, Jade found a positive solution to her social predicament: first, stop then think what the problem is; second, brainstorm different solutions then think of the consequences; third, choose the best solution and take the necessary steps to do it.

Follow up questions and activities for 'A solution to a predicament'

Aims Express emotion using intra-personal processing, interaction, movement and drama.

Think of a time when you wanted to do two things at once. What made you choose one thing instead of another?

Using your own body to make a movement, show how you felt when you chose one thing over another.

In groups of three to six, think of a different ending to the story.

Each group acts out its different story to all the other groups.

Worksheet 13 can be used with story 9.

Story 10
Sadness

Dana was a 16 year old who seemed to be like any other child until she became a teenager. Then, it became clear that she did not have any girlfriends, was constantly tired, did not eat properly and was continuously sad, sleeping with one boyfriend after another. Dana was unaware of what really made her happy and content. She went to her doctor who diagnosed Dana as suffering from depression which was exacerbated by her recent break-up with her boyfriend. She revealed to her doctor that she was thinking of killing herself.

The doctor referred Dana to a therapist who specialized in dealing with teenagers' emotional problems. The therapist listened to Dana explain how she only wanted to get to know boys better but instead ended up sleeping with them, even though she did not feel comfortable about it. Dana also revealed that she did not know how to make friends and that she had just moved to a new school and wanted to know what to say to the other girls after the initial, 'Hello, how are you?'

The therapist's treatment programme focused on teaching Dana how to develop friendships, feel confident with her peers, be assertive, put up boundaries regarding sexual contact, express her emotions appropriately and build intimacy into her life. Consequently, Dana's depression lifted. She no longer carried that deep sadness inside her.

(For a more comprehensive version of the above true story, see *The Case of Dana* from Laura Myson et al.; *Interpersonal Psychotherapy for Depressed Adolescence* published in New York by Guilford Press in 1993.)

Follow up questions and activities for 'Sadness'

Aims   to problem-solve using intra-personal processing, interaction and art.

In groups, brainstorm positive, negative, possible and impossible ways of helping Dana.
After brainstorming, think about what may be possible and what impossible, out of all the ideas brainstormed.
Disregard all the impossible and negative ways suggested.
For the possible and positive suggestions left, work out a helpful programme for Dana, imagining you are the therapist designing a treatment programme for her.
Imagine that you are to send Dana an uplifting illustration. Draw it.

Worksheet 14 can be used with story 10.

Story 11
Jealousy

Pretty Linda seemed an average kind of girl on the outside, but on the inside she felt different. She didn't know what she wanted so would just smile and do what the others wanted. The person she wanted to please most of all was Harry. All she seemed to focus on was being with Harry. If you were to ask Linda, 'When do you feel happy?' or 'What makes you feel content?' she would be silent for a while, smile and then mumble, 'I don't know.' Others ended up feeling fed up with this side of Linda's character and so did Harry. They wanted to know the real Linda behind the smile. Jo was Harry and Linda's mutual friend. He invited Harry to a sleepover party and told Harry he could bring any friend he wanted with him. He also invited Linda and told her she could come to the party with a friend if she wanted to bring one.

They say the colour of jealousy is green, the colour of a cat's eyes. I do not know why (perhaps someone else does). When Harry took Mary to the party instead of Linda, Linda's inner feeling of being different intensified and she was neither happy nor content. She could not put a word to her emotion, although it seems easy to guess that it was jealousy, but she wore her green satin dress and went to Jo's party anyway. During the evening she watched Harry and Mary dancing, never letting them see her. Even though she was in a room full of people, Linda looked lonely and isolated. All the time she wished she was in his arms instead. Linda eventually became tired of standing so she found a space on a settee to sit on and eventually fell asleep there. By the time she woke up, Harry and Mary had gone. Jo said that Mary's mother had come to pick her up shortly after Linda fell asleep and that Harry left early to do his paper round. Did Linda feel any better? She did not know.

Follow up questions and activities for 'Jealousy'

Aims Problem-solve, understand others, being positive and knowing the difference between appropriate and inappropriate behaviour, using intra-personal processing, interaction and drama.

Why do you think people get jealous?
What can you do if you feel lonely?
Think of a different ending to the above short story and share that thought with another person.
Write the story with your different ending as a story board.
In a small group, act out what is on the story board.

Worksheets 15 and 16 can be used with story 11.

Story 12
Pride

One afternoon, Keri walked contentedly home from school. As usual, she took a bar of chocolate and an apple before sitting in front of the television set. Her favourite programmes were cartoons. She watched an advertisement that showed what to do to be involved in helping animals at a special centre. Feeling enthusiastic about being with animals, Keri dialled the telephone number that was advertised. Keri asked the woman who answered the telephone, 'Please can I help at the special animal centre?' After having a few questions answered, the lady said that because Keri was under 14 years old, it would not be possible for her to have a paid job, but she could sometimes come in to help the animals on a voluntary basis.

On Monday after school Keri started her voluntary help with the animals. During that week, she rode to the centre every day after school with a happy heart. She not only became skilled at taking care of animals, but also loved them more and more. One day, Keri sensed that a cat named Sharon was going to have kittens. Sharon did give birth and Keri was unobtrusively there in case her help was needed. The birth went smoothly apart from the final kitten, so the mother needed some help. Keri acted promptly and helped to deliver the kitten with a veterinary surgeon. That day, she flew home feeling proud of herself. Keri told her parents how she helped with the birth of the kitten. They felt very proud of her.

Keri decided that she wanted to be a vet. Her teachers told her she would have to do better with her marks at school to have any hope of being accepted on a veterinary course. Although Keri preferred watching television and playing with kittens to doing homework, she decided it was worth doing it first so that she could eventually be good enough to become a vet. Her perseverance at working hard with schoolwork was rewarded in the end. Keri grew into an intelligent and caring young woman who became a brilliant vet and took pride in doing exceptionally good work.

(This story was inspired by Sophie I. Rudd and Maria C. Rudd)

Follow up questions and activities for 'Pride'

Aims Identifying what one is good at while recognizing how one feels about that, identify with the emotions of others, become more self aware and verbalise a cognitive process as well as communicate non-verbally, using intra-personal processing, interaction and movement.

Why did Keri feel proud?
Think about what you can take pride in. How does it make you feel?

Tell a partner what you are good at.
Move around in such a way which shows that you feel proud.
Write your own story entitled 'Pride'.

Worksheets 17 and 18 can be used with story 12.

Story 13
Guilt

Josephina and Andrea were 17 year old non-identical twins. They excitedly reminded their parents, Mr and Mrs Bates, 'It's your weekend away tomorrow while we house-sit!' Soon, tomorrow became today! They received these seven written rules which they promised to keep, before their mother and father drove to a hotel for a romantic weekend together:

1   You are allowed a maximum of one friend each to stay for the whole weekend.
2   No males in the house until we return.
3   The money we've left with you is only in case of emergency.
4   You can have as many drinks as you like, as long as they are non-alcoholic.
5   Ensure that the house is safely locked before you go to bed.
6   Contact Mr and Mrs Jen next door if you need anything.
7   Telephone us any time you want, either on the mobile or at the hotel.

Josephina's friend Linda and Andrea's friend Sue came to stay at the house. The four friends waved the adults goodbye from the front door, then ran giggling back inside the house. It did not take very long for Sue and Linda to persuade the twins to have a little party. They ignored their fleeting gut feelings of guilt and eagerly telephoned their college friends Oliver, Peter, Adam, Billy, Isabelle and Charlotte, inviting them to come and watch DVDs with them. Then the girls quickly put on their 'cool' clothes and make-up while happily chatting.

The boys arrived altogether with a few other boys and the girls arrived with several others, as news that there was a party without adults on the premises quickly spread.

That little feeling of guilt was now gently knocking on the twins' hearts, but they ignored it. The twins' friends brought alcohol with them – bottles of beer and some vodka. Josephina and Andrea enjoyed having their friends with them and they all had a fun time watching DVDs, eating junk food (which was bought with the emergency money) and talking together. Unfortunately, Isabelle drank too much alcohol and became drunk, which worried Josephina and Andrea very much because they were not sure how to look after her later on when she was feeling very ill. Also, the girls became scared when the boys would not leave to go home but kept pestering the girls instead. Indeed, Oliver became nasty and pushed himself onto Josephina who was terrified that he would rape her. Peter, however, pulled Oliver off her. Then the boys became aggressive, went into the garden shouting at each other and started to fight. The party had become a living nightmare for the twins who now felt very guilty for breaking the rules they had agreed with their parents.

By this time, Josephina and Andrea desperately wanted Oliver, Peter, Adam, Billy, Isabelle and Charlotte to go to their own homes. Charlotte went, but Isabelle lay asleep on the settee. However, the boys would not go away and neither the twins nor their respective friends knew how to make them leave. Andrea started to cry. The twins, Linda and Sue decided that the girls should take it in turns to watch Isabelle all night in case she vomited and died from inhaling it.

They put her in the recovery position and started to watch over her as agreed, while the boys were violently out of control and seemed to surround the house. Mr and Mrs Jen next door heard the commotion and came out to see what was happening.

Feeling concern for the youngsters, the couple ensured that the boys went to their own homes, before telephoning Isabelle's parents to come and pick her up.

Josephina and Andrea had very little sleep that night. Linda and Sue went home early the next morning and the twins spent the day feeling very guilty and making the house look all clean and tidy before their parents came home. Meanwhile, the neighbours and Isabelle's mother telephoned the twins' parents on the mobile and told them what had happened. The news deeply disturbed Mr and Mrs Bates so they rushed home, feeling betrayed by their guilt-ridden twins.

It is up to you, reader, to imagine what happened next.

This story is adapted from a real life situation, so identifying details of individuals have been changed for confidentiality reasons.

Follow up questions and activities for 'Guilt'

Aims   Manage emotions, problem-solve while keeping sight of own needs, pinpoint the difference between needs and wants and perceive a situation from another person's point of view using intra-personal processing, interaction and movement.

What makes people feel guilty?
Think about how a person could live a guilt-free life and write down your ideas
What are your needs? Take turns to tell another person and listen to her or his needs.
What are your wants? Take turns to tell another person and listen to her or his wants. Clarify the difference between 'needs' and 'wants'. Were any of your needs really wants?
Write your own story entitled 'Guilt'. Include actions, emotions and thoughts in your story.
How do you think Mr and Mrs Bates should react to the twins?
What would you do if you were one of the twins?
Look at your partner while having a guilty expression on your face, then change your expression to one of relief. How do you think your partner felt when you changed from one expression to another?
When have you felt guilty and what helped you get over it?

Worksheet 19 can be used with story 13.

Story 14
Anxiety

Lara had a calm exterior. This hid her rapid heart rate, escalating blood pressure and sweating body. As a child, she learnt to show unflappability to survive a difficult situation in her home. The situation was that her mother was an alcoholic and every person in the family ignored that fact. No-one knew how to communicate well in her family, including Lara. Now that she was in her late teens and faced with the undesirable situation of having failed her college exams, she appeared calm, yet her anxiety about which direction she should choose to go in her life manifested physically (sweating with relatively high blood pressure and heart rate).

Eventually, she went to her family doctor because the sudden bursts of rapid heartbeats made her feel tormented. The doctor recommended a specialist who taught Lara how to face her problems and manage them in a healthy way. Consequently, she became a healthier person.

Follow up questions and activities for 'Anxiety'

Aims   Positive self-talk and problem-solve and feel secure using intra-personal processing, interaction and drama.

What helps you feel secure?
Does security reduce anxiety or not?
What can you say to yourself to help you feel better?
What do you think the specialist suggested to Lara?
In pairs, brainstorm ways to help Lara.
Join another pair to make a group of four and share your ideas on helping Lara.
With your group, act out one of the ideas for helping Lara.

Worksheets 20 and 21 can be used with story 14.

Story 15
Alcohol

One day, 13-year-old Duncan met his friends in the park. They all secretly drank alcohol. Duncan's friends went home one by one, but he felt sleepy and lay on the ground in the park. His parents were worried about him because it was getting late and he was not at home. His mother and father went out looking for him, after ringing his friends to try and find out where he was. They found him lying down in the park smelling of alcohol, which worried them very much because they thought that he might be unconscious due to alcohol poisoning. His parents successfully woke him up. When they arrived at their house, Duncan's parents took him to his bed. Then he was sick. His parents wondered, 'Why doesn't he co-operate with us and tell us who he's with, where he goes and what he does?'

Follow up questions and activities for 'Alcohol'

Aims Understand another person's perspective, problem solve, develop listening skills and realize the difference between emotions and actions, using intra-personal processing, interaction and art.

Discuss with a partner: If you were Duncan's parents, what would you do? How do you think Duncan's parents felt when they thought their son was unconscious? Discuss your thoughts with your partner.
What do you think that friends of Duncan's parents might think of Duncan and his parents? Discuss with your partner.

Design a poster showing alcohol abuse dangers.

Worksheets 22 and 23 can be used with story 15.

Plans for using the worksheets

Although worksheets can be used independently, they relate to the preceding stories.

Sheets and activities for Zak's story can be found later, at the end of the numbered and titled worksheets because the activities are an integral part of the (work)sheets as well as the story of Zak. Each of these later worksheets can cover a complete lesson or session. So each worksheet is called a 'session'. They deal with aspects related to Zak's story about a teenager experiencing difficulty in dealing with his emotions and behaviour. Each sheet containing part of Zak's story is also a worksheet that has space for teenagers to work on it.

Those working with teens can use the sheets as part of therapy, PSHE or during Circle Time, to have a way of balancing other studies such as academic work which the teenagers may be involved in, and highlight emotional issues. Sessions sheets provide further expansion of emotional issues, such as stress and depression, and how these effect individuals and those around them; especially the family. Do males and females react to stress and depression in different ways? (Gray, 1992). Zak's story, intended as a stimulus for further work and discussion, offers food for thought on this issue. Ten sessions make a programme. Follow it in sequence. How long it takes depends on how much supplementary work is deemed appropriate.

Creativity

Draw anything you like, using the rectangle as part of your drawing.

What strong or weak emotions do you feel while doing the drawing?

Take it in turns to discuss your emotions with a partner, talk about how you deal with them and if there are better ways of coping with the feelings you pinpointed.

Responsibility

Mum's gone to work and dad's washing up. What should Anne do with the baby? Write your answer in the empty space.

Sad

Draw a sad mouth and tears on Jo's face.

Think of a time when you felt sad.

What helped you cope? Write your answers in the empty space.

Controlling yourself

Your favourite cake is on the kitchen table, but you have not had your main meal yet.
How can you control yourself so that you do not eat the cake immediately?
Write your ideas on this sheet, on each slice of cake.

Self-control

Finish the sentence: You feel annoyed that your tutor has given you detention for being late and you want to shout back at him; instead, you use self-control responding appropriately by

_____

_____

Problem solving

Think of a problem you have. What would you like the solution to be? In the space provided write down the first small step you can take to solve your problem. Then, write down further small achievable steps you can take to solve the problem.

Problem...

Teen + 10 years

Ponder on the question: Where will you be in ten years?

Finish the sentence:

In ten years I will…

Positive response to a negative comment

Read the sentence in the bottom speech bubble.

Fill in the top speech bubble.

Worksheet 9

My contact

If I need to talk to someone, I can contact …
(finish the sentence by filling in the big think bubble) …

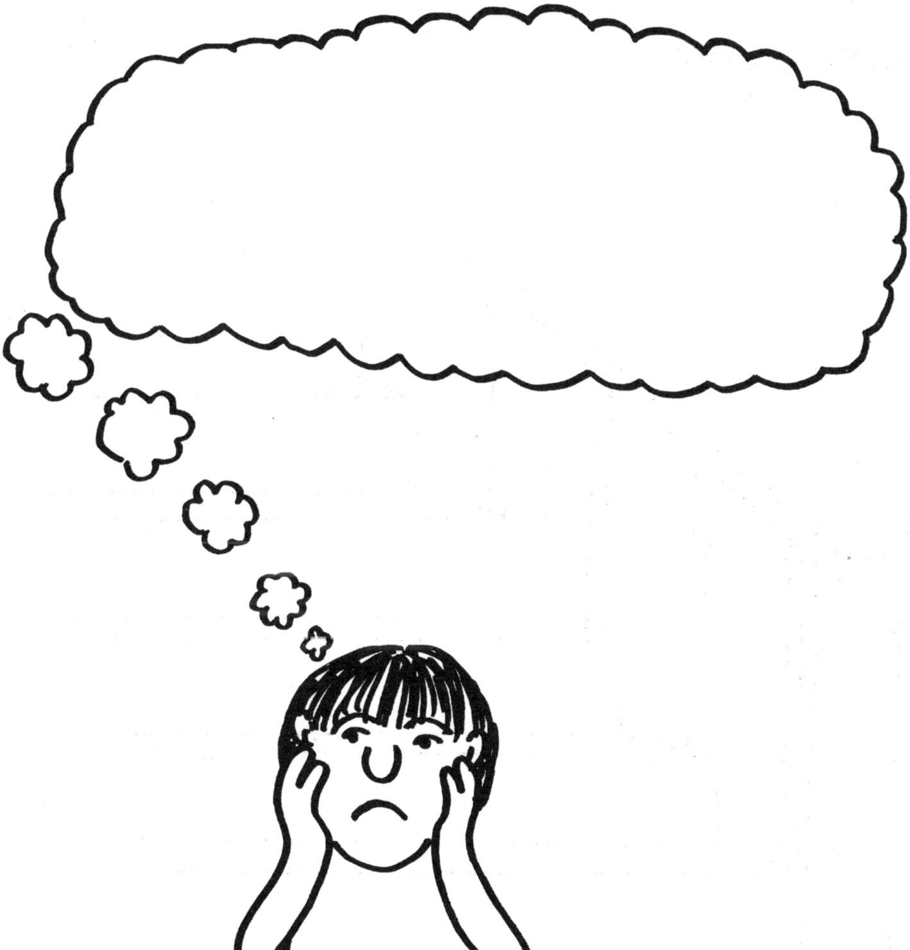

Worksheet 10

10 My life story

On each step, draw a situation that has influenced you or write the individuals' names who have influenced you.

Discuss.

How do you feel?

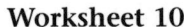

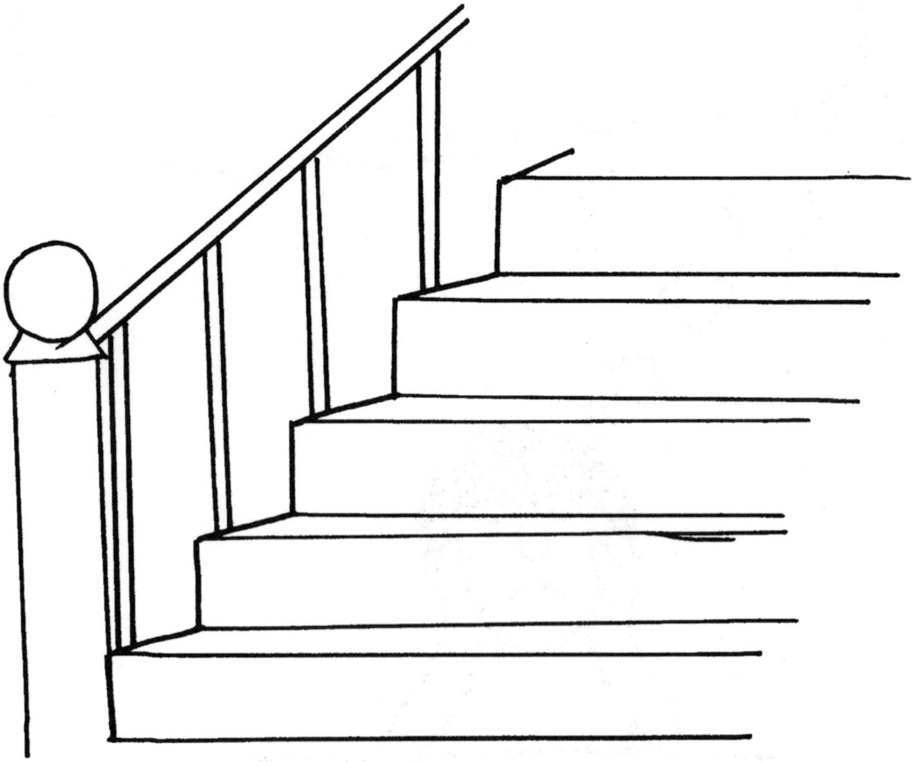

Impulse control

Bev has angrily flared up at Jim for pushing in front of her. How can she relax a little, detract herself from retaliation and defuse her anger? Write your ideas in the boxes.

To relax

To detract

To defuse

Managing anger

Mario is feeling angry and does not know how to calm down. On the lines, write down some of the ways that angry Mario can use to calm down.

Choices

You accept a babysitting job then you are invited for a date on the same evening. Write down three choices that you have, in the mobile phones' text boxes. What should you do? What would you do?

Positive

Inside each hat write down what makes you feel positive and content.

Lonely

Elizabeth has started at a new college and is feeling lonely because she does not know anyone. With a partner take turns to write down what she can do in each book that has fallen out of her bag.

Matching Emotions

What makes you happy or sad?
Draw a sad face in the empty moon shape on the left side of the page and write the word 'sad' in the opposite star.
Name the emotion inside each moon shape and write it in the appropriate opposite empty star.

Self-booster

On each line, write something that you like about yourself.

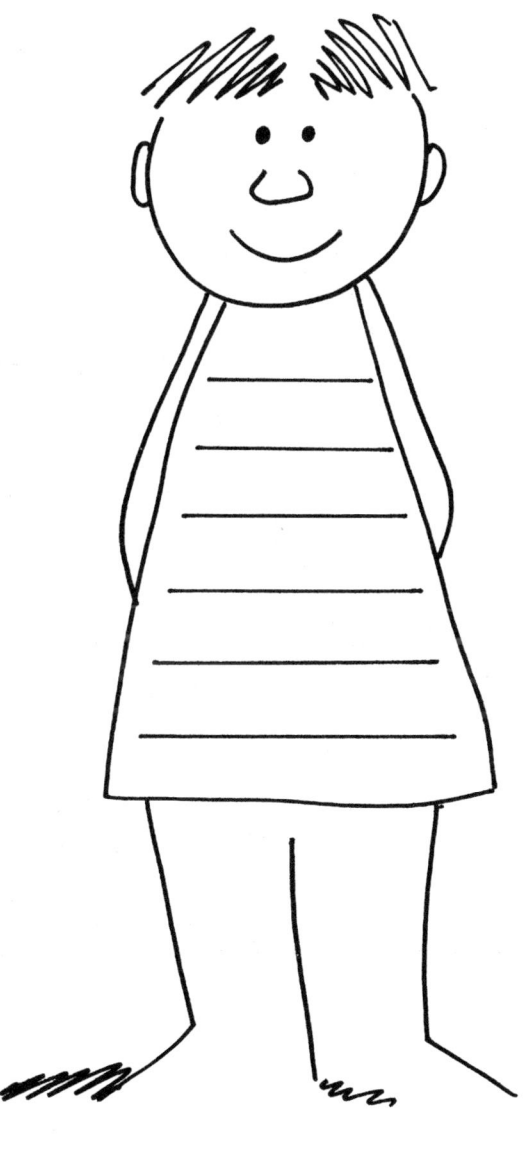

Affirmations

On each paving stone write or draw something that you are good at.

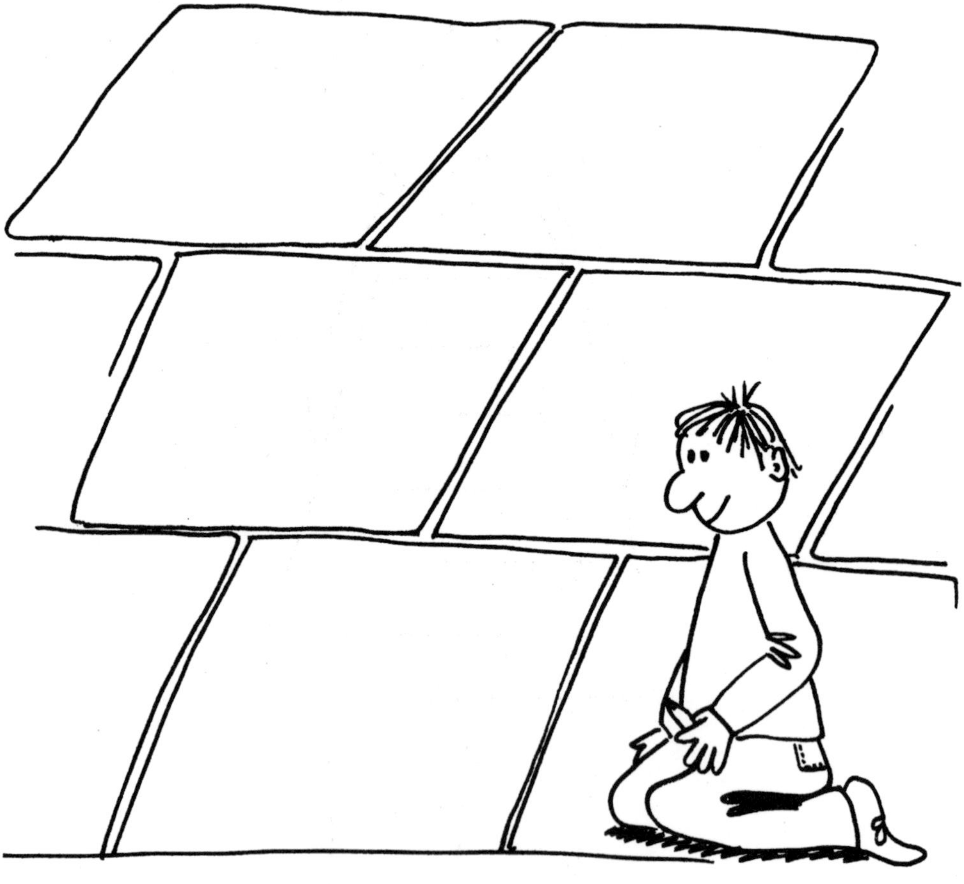

Self-concept

Inside each letter, write a short sentence starting 'I am'. For example, 'I am a teenager.'

THIS IS ME!

Understand and manage emotions

Mario misses his bus so arrives home feeling hot and angry. He has a relaxing bath. In the empty shapes on this worksheet, draw and write down other things that he can do to feel better.

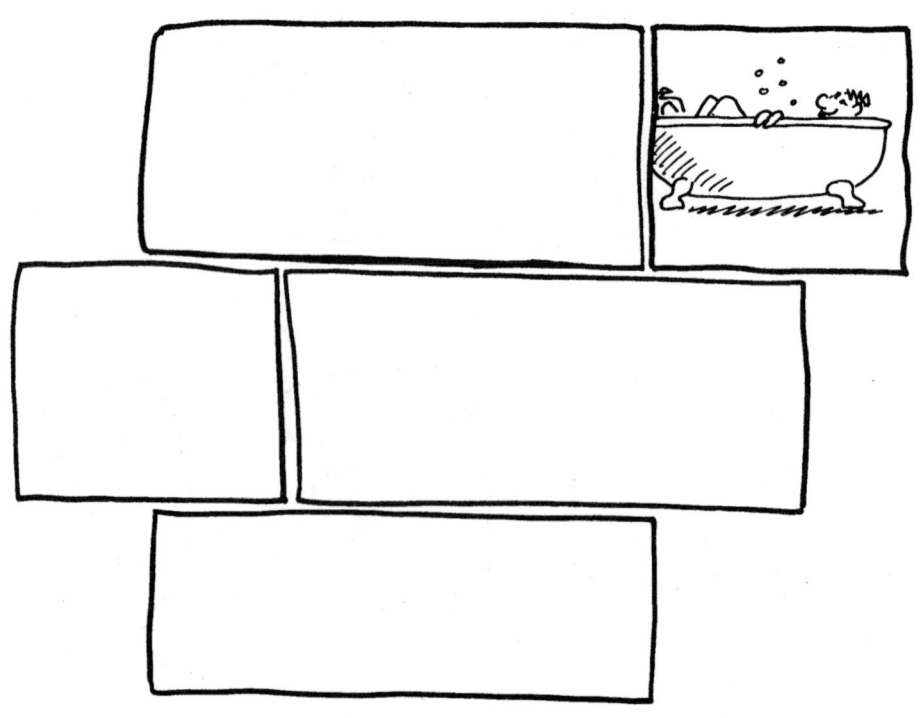

Communication

A person who is a good communicator has the following skills:

_____

_____

A time I communicated well was:

_____

_____

Compliments

Think of someone you care about. In each ray of sunshine, write something that you like about the person. Put the person's name on the lines in the sun's centre.

Co-operation

Sita and Eurjon come from different cultural backgrounds. Unfortunately, Sita's family disapprove of Eurjon and Eurjon's family disapprove of Sita. Indeed, Eurjon's family want to arrange a marriage for him. Discuss the pros and cons of having an arranged marriage. How do you think Sita and Eurjon feel? Write your responses in the empty space.

Session 1

1) On your own, think what a 15-year-old girl might find stressful.

2) Share your views with a partner.

3) Write down the issues raised on each of your work sheets.

Issues raised:

_____

_____

_____

_____

Zak was unaware of the sun shining on his home

Alone with his negative thoughts, he didn't notice the leafy tree,

or the blooming flowers.

Session 1 Activities

Assuming Zak is 14, what could be distressing him?

In groups of four to six, brainstorm what might have happened before the first illustration on this page.

In your groups, take 10 minutes to work out a 2 minute playlet about Zak's distress.

Each group perform, your playlet to the others.

Discuss the playlets as a whole.

Illustrate a continuation of Zak's story, with commentary, in the three empty triangles within 'session 1 activities'.

Session 2

1) On your own, think of one person who cares about you.

2) On your own, think of two people you care about.

3) On your own, think of three people Zak might care about.

4) How do you think those three people would feel if they saw Zak crying?

Person 1	Person 2	Person 3

Tears rolled down his cheeks. Feeling bad about himself, Zak was unable to cope with his problem.

He didn't even smile at his happy little sister

who tried to cheer him up with a balloon.

Session 2 Activities

What do you think Zak's private thoughts are? Discuss this with a partner.

What do you think his sister's private thoughts are? Discuss this with a partner.

In the space provided within empty rectangles, write down private thoughts, which correspond with the illustration that you draw above each one of them.

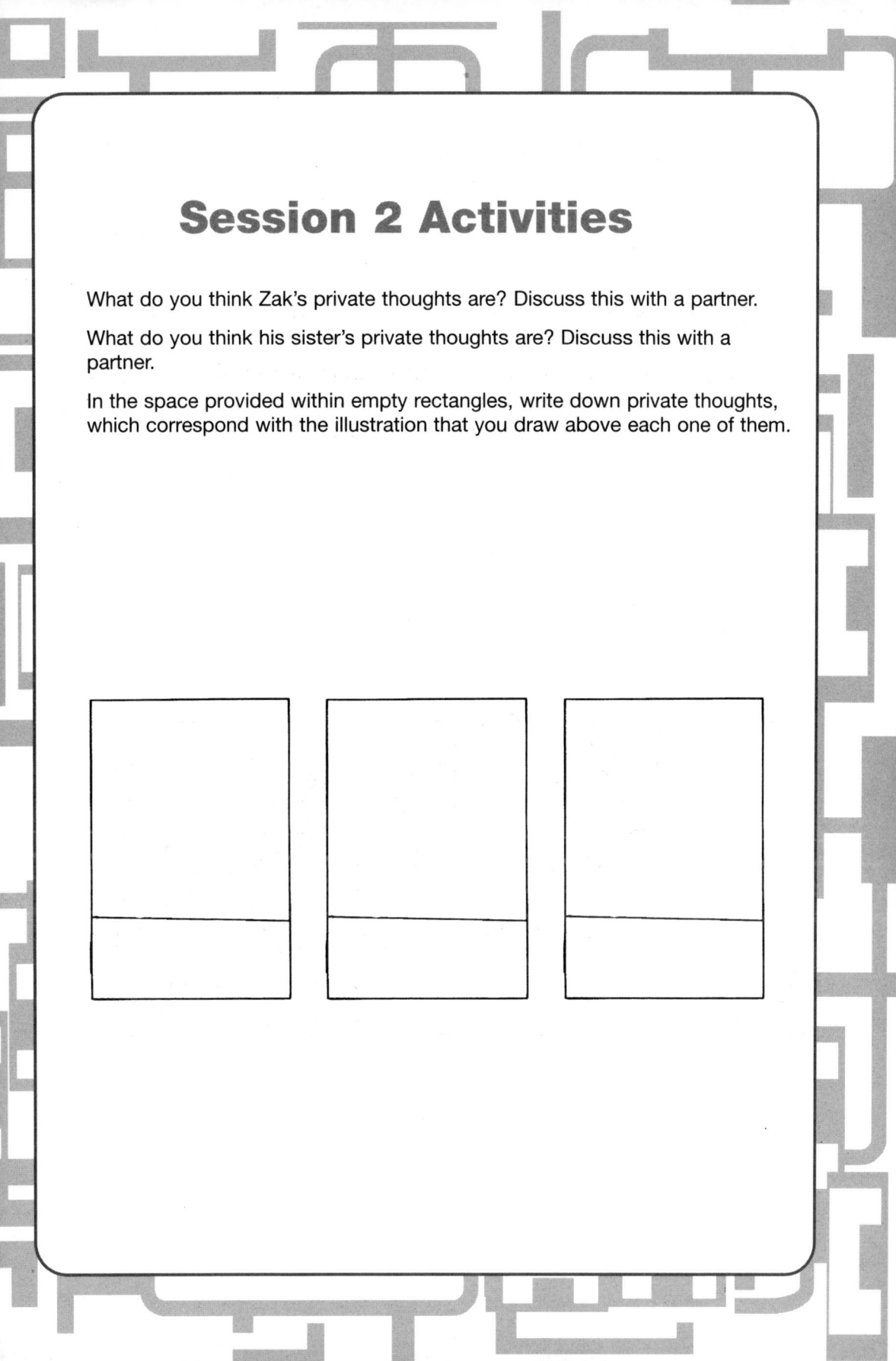

Session 3

1) In pairs, discuss how you think Zak's father feels about him, with reference to the middle illustration on this page.

2) In your pairs, think of ways Zak's father might help Zak to feel loved, wanted and respected.

3) Write down how to put these ways into action.

"A joke'll cheer you up!" declared Zak's dad, while holding a balloon for his daughter Katy.

"Good idea," said Arthur, Zak's brother.

"No!" exclaimed Zak, while turning his back on his loved ones. Arthur then gave Katy a shoulder ride.

Session 3 Activities

In groups of four to six, brainstorm ways you can help someone you care about feel loved, wanted and respected.

In your groups, take ten minutes to work out a 2 minute playlet on helping Zak to feel loved, wanted and respected.

Each group perform to the others.

Make a story-board of your playlet.

Session 4

1) In pairs, discuss what Zak is like from his mother's point of view.

2) Stay in your pairs and discuss what Zak is like from his father's point of view.

3) Write down two different points of view about Zak.

1 _____

_____

2 _____

_____

"Give me a piggy-back now!" shouted Katy, as Arthur went to look for his mum.

Zak's stepmother came into the garden saying, "I know who can help".

"Let's get in the car and go for some talking therapy," she continued.

Session 4 Activities

In the first empty rectangle draw one person that Zak could go to for support and write down who that person is.

In the second and third empty rectangles draw two (one in each) more people Zak could go to for support and write down who they are.

Session 5

1) In pairs, discuss what Zak is like from his sister's point of view.

2) Stay in your pairs and discuss what Zak is like from his brother's point of view.

3) Write down a point of view his sister may have and a point of view his brother may have about him.

She made an appointment for the family, who drove to their session of talking therapy.

They soon found the building. The psychologist's name was Mr. Owkai.

Mr. Owkai had a rather comfortable reception room where the family waited.

Session 5 Activities

If Zak were a sort of weather, what would the weather be? Draw this sort of weather in the first rectangle.

If Zak's mother was a type of weather, what would that weather be? Draw this sort of weather in the second rectangle.

Draw your favourite weather in the third rectangle.

Session 6

1) Zak's family are waiting in the reception room for the family therapist. Do you think that the environment makes them feel better or worse?

2) In groups of up to six people, discuss your views and reach your decisions.

3) Write down your decisions with reasons why you chose them.

1 _____

2 _____

3 _____

A small lady came out of Mr. Owkai's consulting room.

An old man followed her.

Finally, a very young woman with a baby followed him.
All were smiling.

Session 6 Activities

In the first rectangle, draw an environment which would not please you.

In the second rectangle draw an environment which would please you.

In the third rectangle write your reasons for choosing these two environments.

Session 7

1) In pairs, discuss a problem that might have made Zak's family visit a therapist.

2) In pairs, discuss what you would do with the problem.

3) Brainstorm solutions to the problem and write them down.

4) Create a best plan with your partner.

5) Write down all the reasons that you and your partner can think of, why the plan might work.

_____

_____

_____

_____

"Mr. Owkai will see you now," announced his fair-haired assistant.

"Well," said Mr. Owkai calmly looking at the family, "you'll be o.k.".

They all sat in a circle, answering Mr. Owkai's questions about each other and feeling understood.

Session 7 Activities

In the first rectangle, write down one problem that a 17-year-old girl might have; illustrate this if you wish.

In the second rectangle, write down who can support the girl with the problem; illustrate this if you wish.

In the third rectangle, write down as many solutions to the problem that you can find.

Decide on the best plan.

Session 8

1) Identify the feeling Zak's family might have at the end of the therapy session.

2) Find a partner and each of you listen to one another as you describe the feeling you identified.

3) Have you ever had that feeling? If so, explain what happened to your partner; take turns in listening.

"Thank you Mr. Owkai", said Zak, looking joyful.

Zak and his family went home in their car. Zak felt empowered.

He even winked at a pretty young lady on the pavement.

In the empty space, draw a situation where Zak and or his family are doing the 'wrong' thing, or something inappropriate which makes Zak worse.

Discuss your drawing with a partner.

Session 9

1) In pairs, think about what enabled Zak to calm down and stop his problematic way of thinking and behaving? Discuss this before pooling your ideas and writing them down.

2) Who chose to go to the family therapist?

3) Describe the consequence of this choice.

He even blew a wolf-whistle at a flower lady who blushed.

At home, Zak gave Katy a balloon. He knew she'd like it.

It seemed to him, that for the first time, he noticed what a lovely day it was.

In the empty space, draw and then describe a situation that energises you, makes you feel positive and also more aware of your surroundings:

Session 10

In comic-strip style, use the top row of rectangles to draw a story-line of a person who is a bad communicator. Use the smaller rectangles for commentary.

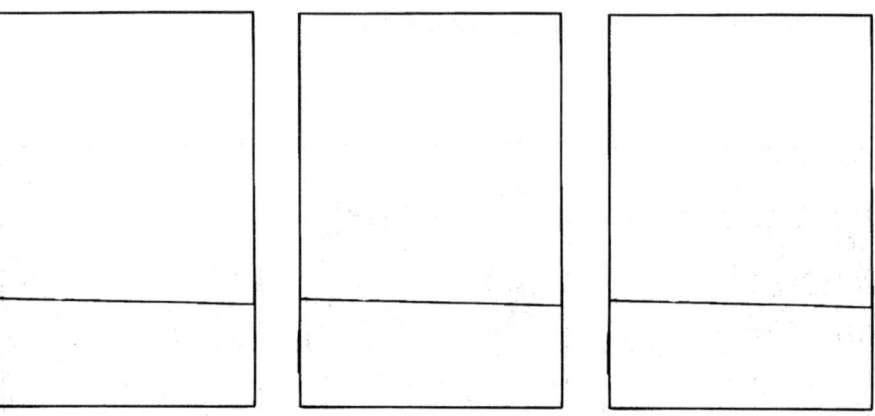

Within the next three empty rectangles, use a comic-strip style to draw a story-line of a person who is good at communciating. Use the smaller rectangels for commentary.

References

Apter, T. (1997) *The Confident Child*. London: Norton.

Baker, P. (1998) *Here's Health*. March: 20–22.

Batmanghelidijh, C. (2007) 'There is nowhere to hide', *Counselling Psychology Review, 22* (3): 55–59.

Bayne, R., Horton, I., Merry, A. and Noyes, E. (1993) *The Counsellor's Handbook*. London: Chapman Hall.

Berne, E. (1964) *Games People Play – the Psychology of Human Relationships*. New York: Grove Press.

Berne, E. (1970) *Sex in Human Loving*. New York: Simon and Schuster.

Bliss, T., Robinson, G. and Maines, B. (1995) *Developing Circle Time*. Bristol: Lucky Duck.

Brady, R., Bacon, J. and Ryves, D. (2000) 'A case study illustrating potent adverse impact in two popular psychometric ability tests', *Selection Development Review, 16* (4): 10–15.

Brooking-Payne, K. (1996) *Games Children Play, How Games and Sport Help Children Develop*. Stroud: Hawthorn Press.

Brown, J. (1998) *Large-scale Health Promotion Stress Workshops: Promotion and Client Response*. Brighton 1998 British Psychological Society annual conference: unpublished paper presentation.

Butler, G. and Hope, T. (1997) *Manage your Mind, The Mental Fitness Guide*. Oxford: Oxford University Press.

Chopra, D. (1993) *Ageless Body Timeless Mind*. London: Rider.

Cooper, S. and Willis, L. in K. Brooking-Payne (1996) *Games Children Play, How Games and Sport Help Children Develop*. Stroud: Hawthorn Press.

Cross, J., Kaplan, L., Gurner, A., Jackson, S., Maines, B., Clemson, S., Walker, S., Sidebottom, D., Hill, J., Sanday, H., Marson, P., Wardle, C. and Stinchcombe, V. (2000) *The Emotional Literacy Hour*. Bristol: Lucky Duck.

Cole, T. (1998) 'Peer support new beginnings in Japan', *Peer Support Network*, Issue 9: 3–4.

Cowie, H. (1998) Editorial, *Peer Support Networker*, Issue 9: 1.

Dixon, R. (1998) 'Interventions across Europe to combat bullying; A personal view' *Peer Support Networker*, Issue 9: 3–4.

Denham, S. A. and Burton, R. (1996) 'A social-emotional intervention for at-risk-4-year-olds' *Journal of School Psychology, 34* (3): 225–245.

Domitrovich, C. E., Cortes, R. and Greenberg, M. T. (2002, June) *Preschool PATHS: Promoting social and emotional competence in young children*. Paper presented at the 6th National Head Start Research Conference: Washington, DC.

Douglas, B. (2007) 'Conference Plenary Summary', *Counselling Psychology Review, 2* (3): 69–70.

Emerson, R. W. (1803–1882) http://www.transcendentalists.com/1emerson.html

Gardner, H. (1993) *Multiple Intelligences: The Theory in Practice*. New York: Basic Books.

Gerhardt, S. (2004) *Why Love Matters*. London: Brumer-Routledge.

Gerhardt, S. (2007) 'Making a Person: The lasting impact of babyhood' *Counselling Psychology Review, 22* (3): 37–44.

Goleman, D. (1995) *Emotional Literacy: Why it matters more than IQ*. New York: Bantam.

Goleman, D. (1996) *Emotional Intelligence*. London: Bloomsbury.

Goleman, D. (2004) *Destructive Emotions and How we can Overcome Them, A Dialogue with the Dalai Lama*. London: Bloomsbury.

Gottman, J. (1998) *The Heart of Parenting*. London: Bloomsbury.

Grant, W. T. (1992) 'Consortium on the School-Based Promotion of Social Competence, Drug and Alcohol Prevention Curricula', in J. D. Hawkins, et al (1992) *Communities that Care*. San Fransisco: Josey-Bass.

Gray, J. (1992) *Men are from Mars, Women are from Venus*. London: Harper Collins.

Greenberg, M. T. and Kursche, C. A. (1998) 'Preventive interventions for school-age deaf children: The Paths curriculum', *Journal of Deaf Studies and Deaf Education 3* (1): 49–63.

Griffin, J. (2001) *Breaking the Cycle of Depression Without Drugs*. Hailsham: Mindfields.

Griffin, J. and Tyrrell, I. (2001) 'Emotional Knowledge as a predictor of social behaviour and academic competence in children at risk within Psychological Science (2001) 12, 18–23' *Human Givens – Radical Psychology Today (8)*: 3–4.

Gross, J., Kaplan, L., Gurner, A., Jackson, S., Maines, B., Clemson, S., Walker, S., Sidebottom, D., Hill, J., Sanday, H., Marson, P., Wardle, C. and Stinchcombe, V. (2000) *The Emotional Literacy Hour*. Bristol: Lucky Duck Publishing.

Harrill, S. E. (1996) *Empowering Teens to Build Self-esteem*. Houston, Tx: Innerworks Publishing.

Howe, D. (1993) *On Being a Client*. London: Sage.

Jacobs, A. (1973) 'TA and Psychodrama', in M. James, (ed.), *Techniques in Transactional Analysis for Psychotherapists and Counsellors*. Reading MA, Addison- Wesley. pp. 239–249.

James, F. and Brownsword, K. (1994) *A Positive Approach: creating a learning environment that encourages and supports good behaviour*. Twickenham: Belair Publications Limited.

Joseph, G. E. and Strain P. S. (2003a) 'Enhancing emotional vocabulary in young children', *Young Exceptional Children', 6* (4): 16–26.

Joseph, G. E. and Strain, P. S. (2003b) 'Helping young children control anger and handle disappointment', *Young Exceptional Children 7* (1): 21–29.

Kirscherbaum, H. and Henderson, V. (1989) *The Carl Rogers Reader*. CA: Houghton Miffin.

Kusche, C. A. and Greenberg, M. T. (1994) *The PATHS Curriculum*. Seattle, WA: Developmental Research and Programs.

Lesirge, R. (2001a) *I Want to be Your Friend but I Don't Know How to*. London: Mental Health Foundation.

Lesirge, R. (2001b) *Promoting Mental Health in Primary Schools*. London: Mental Health Foundation.

Lindenfield, G. (1994) *Confident Children*. London: Thorsons.

Mair, M. (2001) *Research on Emotions*, unpublished paper presented at the British Psychological Society's Division of Counselling Psychology Conference, England.

Makin, P. and Ruitenbeck, D. V. (1998) *The Psychological Contract as a Close Relationship*. Brighton 1998 British Psychological Society annual conference, unpublished paper presentation.

Martin, P. (1998) *The Psychological Contract as a Close Relationship*. Brighton 1998 British Psychological Society annual conference: unpublished paper presentation.

Mayer, D. J. and Salovey, P. (1993) 'The Intelligence of Emotional Intelligence', *Intelligence Journal 17* (4): 433–443.

McGrellis, S., Thomas, R. Holland, J., Henderson, S. and Sharpe, S. (1998) *Hoping for Heaven: fearing exclusion; the location of young people's fears in time and place*. Brighton 1998 British Psychological Society annual conference: unpublished research paper presentation.

Moore, B. and Beland, K. (1992) *Evaluation of Second Step, pre-school-kindergarten: A violence prevention curriculum kit – Summary report*. Seattle, WA: Committee for Children.

Morrison, B. (1997) *As If*. London: Granta Books.

Mortimer, H. (1998) *Personal and Social Development*. Leamington Spa: Scholastic Limited.

Nilsen, A. (1998) *The Failure as a Nation and a Point of Reference in the Thoughts of Young People*. Brighton 1998 British Psychological Society annual conference: unpublished research paper presentation.

Noeker, M. and Pertermann, F. (1998) 'Children's and adolescents' perception of their asthma bronchial', *Child Care, Health and Development – The Multi-disciplinary Journal, 17* (4): 433–443.

Ollendick, T. H., Matson, J. L., and Helsel, W. J. (1985) 'Fears in children and adolescents: Normative data', *Behaviour, Research and Therapy, 23*: 265–467.

Olsen, R. and Sutton, J. (1998) 'More hassle, more alone: adolescents with diabetes and the role of formal and informal support', *Child Care, Health and Development – The Multi-disciplinary Journal, 24* (1): 21–39.

Perry, B. (2006). *Bonding and Attachment in Maltreated Children; How You Can Help.* Leamington Spa. Scholastic.

Rae, T. (2000) *Dealing with Feeling.* London: Sage.

Rasmussen, P. (2001) *Disruptive Children Thrive After Bing Given a Second Chance.* Birmingham Post, January 19.

Robinson, G. and Maines, B. (1998) *Circle Time Resources.* Bristol: Lucky Duck Publishing.

Rogers, C. (1951) *Client-centred Therapy.* London: Constable.

Rogers, C. (1961) *On Becoming a Person.* London: Constable.

Rudd, B. (1998) *Talking is for Kids – Emotional Literacy for Infant School Children.* Bristol: Lucky Duck Publishing.

Rudd, B. (2000) *Cross-cultural Interpersonal Space in Assumed Counselling Relationships with Same and Opposite Sex Pairs and Counsellors Perspectives on Proxemics.* Unpublished Ph.D. from London, City University.

Rudd, B. K. (2002) *EQ Pack, Connecting Heart with Mind – book and game.* Milton Keynes. Incentive Plus.

Rudd, B. K. (2002a) *Talking is for Us, Emotional literacy for Key Stage 2 children* (1st edn). Bristol: Lucky Duck.

Rudd, B. K. (2003) *Body Mind Update – resource for new health findings.* Uckfield: BodyMind.

Rudd, B. (2005a) *Anger Management Game.* Milton Keynes: Incentive Plus.

Rudd, B. (2005b) *Stress Control Game.* Milton Keynes: Incentive Plus.

Rudd, B. (2006) *EI emotional intelligence series of ten games.* Milton Keynes: Incentive Plus.

Sassoon, D. (2001) 'Classroom Chaos Rules, Not OK', *Human Givens 8* (3): 29–33.

Scherer, M. W. and Nakamura, C. Y. (1968) 'A fear survey schedule for children (FSSC) A factor analytic comparison with manifest anxiety (CMAS)', *Behaviour, Research and Therapy, 6*: 173–182.

Schilling, D. (1996) *Emotional Intelligence Level 1.* Toronto: Innerchoice Publishing.

Schilling, D. (1999) *50 Activities for Teaching Emotional Intelligence – Level III High School.* California: Interchoice Publishing.

Seligman, M. E. P. (2005) *Authentic Happiness – Using the New Positive Psychology to Realize Your Potential for Lasting Fulfilment.* London: Nicholas Brealey Publishing.

Sharon, M. (1998) *Complete Nutrition: How to Live in Total Health.* London: Priori.

Shure, M. B. (2000) *I Can Problem Solve: An inter-personal cognitive problem-solving program.* Champaign, IL: Research Press.

Simons, J. (1998) *Paradoxes in learning and teaching.* Brighton 1998 British Psychological Society annual conference: unpublished paper presentation.

Stacey, H. and Robinson, P. (1997) *Let's Mediate.* Bristol: Lucky Duck Publishing.

Stacey, H. (2001) *Peer Mediation Training for Young People.* Bristol: Lucky Duck Publishing.

Steiner, C. (1996) 'Emotional Literacy Training: the Application of Transactional Analysis to the study of Emotions', *Transactional Analysis Journal, 26* (1): 31–38.

Steiner, C. (1980) 'Radical Psychiatry, Once Again with Feeling', *Issues in Radical Therapy, 25*: 26–31.

Steiner, C. (1997) *Achieving Emotional Literacy – A Program to Increase Emotional Intelligence.* London: Bloomsbury.

Swallow, B. and Romick, R. (1998) *Towards the Millennium: young people's values, beliefs and thoughts*. Brighton 1998 British Psychological Society annual conference: unpublished research paper presentation.

Wallace, F. (1998) *What Else Can I Do With You?* Bristol: Lucky Duck Publishing.

Webster-Stratton, C. (1990) *The Teachers and Children Video-tape Series: Dina dinosaur school*. Seattle, WA: The Incredible Years.

Webster-Stratton, C. (1999) *How to Promote Children's Social and Emotional Competence*. London: Paul Chapman.

Webster-Stratton, C. and Hammond, M. (1997) 'Treating children with early-onset conduct problems: A comparison of child and parent training interventions', *Journal of Consulting and Clinical Psychology 65* (1): 93–109.

Weisinger, H. (1998) *Emotional Intelligence at Work, The Untapped Edge of Success*. CA: Williams.

List of useful resources

Corbin, C. B. (2003) *Concepts of Fitness and Wellness: A Comprehensive Lifestyle Approach.* Berkely: McGraw-Hill.

Greeff, A. (2005) *Resilience, Personal Skills for Effective Learning – Volume 1.* Carmarthen: Crown House Publishing.

Greeff, A. (2005) *Resilience, Personal Skills for Effective Learning – Volume 2.* Carmarthen: Crown House Publishing.

Kaufeldt, M. (2005) *Teachers Change Your Bait.* Carmarthen: Crown House Publishing.

Nezu, A., Nezu, C. and Jain, D. (2005) *The Emotional Wellness Way to Cardiac Health: How letting go of Depression, Anxiety and Anger can Heal Your Heart.* California: New Harbinger Publication.

Osho (2007) *Emotional Wellness – Transforming Fear, Anger and Jealousy into Creative Energy.* New York: Random House.

Parker, H. C. (1999) *Put Yourself in Their Shoes.* FL: Speciality Press Inc.

Subject index

Note: Readers looking for specific stories or worksheets are referred to the Resources index.

academic competence 10
activities *see* stories and activities
affect 3–4
amygdala 7
anger 8
arousal 7
assessment *see* record keeping

behaviour 10
    disruptive 8, 13
    and emotional literacy 4
brain
    activity 7
    plasticity 12–13
Bulger tragedy 14

Circle Time 13, 16
Citizenship sessions 11–12
class teacher *see* teachers
cognition 4
communication skills 4
congruence 4
crying 6–7
cultural activities 7
curriculum
    Government's influence 11–12
    National Curriculum 11–12
    social skills 13
    value of emotional literacy 9, 15

disadvantaged youngsters 10
disruptive behaviour 8, 13

education 9
emotional instincts 7, 13
emotional intelligence 1
    importance 10–11
    and IQ 11
emotional literacy 1, 12
    characteristics/qualities 4–5
    five pillars of 3

emotional literacy *cont.*
    key aspects 3–4
    research and perspectives 10–13
emotions 3–4, 12–13
    brain activity 7
    mental and physical links 6
empathy 4
evidence, collecting 18
exclusions from school 11

fears 8–9
    8–12 year olds 64
five pillars of emotional
        literacy 3
    and planning work 17
Friends Circles 13
funding 14

games 11, 14–15
    4–7 year olds 22
    8–12 year olds 66
    13–19 year olds 115
Government policy 11–12
gratification 4

health 6–8
    stress and resilience 15
homelessness 9
homework 17

illness 9
imagination 8
immunoglobin-A 7
impulses 4
inherited traits 12–13
    emotional instincts 7
insticts *see* inherited traits
interpersonal intelligence 1
IQ
    and emotional arousal 7–8
    vs emotional intelligence 11

journals, professional 14

laughter 6–7
league tables 11
limbic system 7
logic 7
loneliness 9
love 8–9

mental health 9, 13–14
    mental suffering 10
money 14
multiple intelligences 1

National Curriculum 11–12
neocortex 7
non-verbal skills 4

parents
    involvement 14
    links with 17
    parenting classes 12, 13
peer support 5–6
perpetrators 14
planning 17–18
    4–7 year olds 20
    8–12 year olds 64
    13–19 year olds 112–13
    worksheets *see* separate Resources
        index
play 11, 15–16
problem-solving skills 4
professional audience 14–15
PSHE sessions 12
psychoneuroimmunolgy 6–8

reciprocal love 8–9
record keeping and assessment 18
    4–7 year olds 21–3
    8–12 year olds 65–7, 84
    13–19 year olds 114, 115, 117

research and perspectives 10–13, 14
resilience 15
resources *see* separate Resources Index
schemes of work, developing 17–18
    see also planning
schools 9–10
    exclusions 11
    National Curriculum 11–12
self-awareness 4, 6, 16
self-esteem 6
sleep 7
stories and activities
    4–7 year olds 24–29
    8–12 year olds 68–77
    13–19 year olds 116–37
    see also separate Resources Index
stress management 15
support
    by parents and government
        12, 14, 17
    for parents 12, 13

teachers
    information for 14
    role of 5–6
tears 6–7
teenagers 112–13
tolerance 8
truancy 15

unconditional positive regard 4
unemployment 9

verbal skills 4
victims 14

worksheets 17–18
    4–7 year olds 30–7, 38–61
    8–12 year olds 78–83, 84–109
    13–19 year olds 138, 139–78
    see also separate Resources Index

Resources index

TALKING IS FOR KIDS (4–7 year olds)
introduction 20
record keeping and assessment 21–3

stories and activities
1. Jerry goes shopping 24–5
2. Monique and her kitten 26
3. Clever Thomas 27
4. Peter in the playground 28
5. Isabella had a friend 29

worksheets (plans in *italics*)
1. Talking is for kids *30*, 38
2. Hello, I am a helper 39
3. Inside you/Outside world 40
4. Talking isn't medicine *30*, 41
5. Feeling good. Feeling bad (1) 42
6–8. You can feel bad *31*, 43–5
9. Feeling good. Feeling bad (2) *31*, 46
10. Five ways to feel good *32*, 47
11. Healthy mind and body *32–3*, 48
12. Grow strong and healthy *33*, 49
13. Play with friends *34*, 50
14. Grow and heal *34*, 51
17. Balance your life *35–6*, 54
15. Be happy *34–5*, 52
16. Your feelings *35*, 53
17. Balance your life *35–6*, 54
18. Be kind to yourself *36*, 55
19. Feelings 56
20. Jerry goes shopping 57
21. Monique and her kitten 58
22. Clever Thomas 59
23. Feel secure in setting *36–7*, 60
24. Sense of self-worth *37*, 61

TALKING IS FOR US (8–12 year olds)
introduction 64
record keeping and assesment 65–7, 84

stories and activities
1. Cecil and the little creature 68–9
2. The twin 72–3
3. Yoko and the bully 70–1

4. Polyanna's ninth birthday 74–5
5. The school hamster 76–7

worksheets (plans in *italics*)
1. Record of assessment 84
2. Achievement 85
3. Favourite pet *78*, 86
4. Let's talk *79–80*, 91
5. Recognise feelings *80*, 88
6. The present *79–80*, 89
7. Liking and smiling *80*, 90
A–R. Belinda gets help *80–2*, 91–108
S. Self-worth *82*, 109

TALKING IS FOR TEENS
 (13–19 year olds)
introduction 112–13
record keeping and assessment 114

stories and activities
1. Smoking 117
2. Drug abuse 118–20
3. Pregnancy 120–1
4. Dropping out 122
5. Violence 123
6. Disease 124–5
7. Impulse control 126
8. Managing anger 127
9. A solution to a predicament 128–9
10. Sadness 130
11. Jealousy 131
13. Guilt 134–5
14. Anxiety 136
15. Alcohol 137
Zak's story *138*, 164–80

worksheet (plans in *italics*)
1. Creativity 139
2. Responsibility 140
3. Sad 141
4. Controlling yourself 142
5. Self-control 143
6. Problem solving 144
7. Teen + 10 years 145

8. Positive response to a negative comment 146
9. My contact 147
10. My life story 148
11. Impulse control 149
12. Managing anger 150
13. Choices 151
14. Positive 152
15. Lonely 153

16. Matching emotions 154
17. Self-booster 155
18. Affirmations 156
19. Self-concept 157
20. Understand and manage emotions 158
21. Communication 159
22. Compliments 160
23. Co-operation 161
Zak's story *138*, 162–78